It is said that the number one problem of twenty-first-century man is an identity crisis. From my many years of counseling and training thousands in self-development, I would agree that this crisis is critical. *The Image Maker* is a masterpiece toward helping us solve this challenge. Terry Crist has made his mark with this exceptional work. Everyone should read this one.

—Dr. Myles Munroe, Senior Pastor
Bahamas Faith Ministries International
Founder of The Diplomat Center

With the skill of a wordsmith and the research of a teacher, Terry Crist uncovers truth regarding our being "made in the image of God." He chips away at what doesn't belong and, like a master sculptor, leaves only what is needed. The result of reading this book should be a restoration of self-worth without pride.

—Tommy Tenney, Founder of the GodChasers Network
Author of *The God Chasers* and *God's Dream Team*

The Image Maker may well be one of the most important books of this generation. In a world that knows that the lack of self-esteem means ultimate failure, we look in vain for an image of ourselves that will give our lives fulfillment, purpose, meaning and success. Never before have I read a manuscript that describes the radical nature of the new birth as does this one. It is this experience that gives us our true self-worth based upon who you are in Christ—not a self-esteem based upon your performance. *The Image Maker* is the book that had to be written and the book that must be read!

—Tommy Reid, Senior Pastor
The Tabernacle, Buffalo, NY

Your vision for *The Image Maker*, to awaken believers to the beauty of union with Christ and the security that comes in identifying with Him, was academically, professionally, scripturally and spiritually accomplished. I finished the manuscript wanting more! Your book brings the power of Christ's atoning work for all who dare to believe. I believe every "born of the Spirit" person should be given a copy of this book to read to help them continue to walk in their union with Christ.

—Dr. Dianne McIntosh, Ph.D.
The Grace Ministry

D1414557

Terry Crist brilliantly navigates us through the turbulent waters of the self-esteem movement. With biblical insight and heartfelt inspiration, we discover the wonder of God and the magnificent worth of those who bear His image. This is a life-changing book.

—TOM MOFFETT, SENIOR PASTOR
EVANGELISTIC TEMPLE, HOUSTON, TX

Be free to accept that you are fearfully and wonderfully made. In Terry Crist's new book, *The Image Maker*, you will discover that as a child of God you can be delivered from insignificance and insecurity. Written with a prophetic edge that speaks straight to your heart, this book will loose you to discover the true you. You can become who you really are.

—JOHN MASON
AUTHOR OF *AN ENEMY CALLED AVERAGE* AND
YOU'RE AN ORIGINAL, DON'T DIE A COPY

A deep and far-reaching study on personal image and destiny.

—COLIN DYE, SENIOR PASTOR
KENSINGTON TEMPLE, LONDON, ENGLAND

The Image Maker is a gourmet meal of spiritual and intelligent thought from the heart and soul of Terry Crist. There are books that bless and encourage, and there are books that can change a life. Read this book carefully. There is change between the pages!

—DICK BERNAL, FOUNDER/SENIOR PASTOR
JUBILEE CHRISTIAN CENTER
SAN JOSE, CA

THE IMAGE MAKER

CREATION
H O U S E

II COR. 5:16-17

Signed by the Author

THE IMAGE MAKER

TERRY M. CRIST

THE IMAGE MAKER by Terry M. Crist
Published by Creation House
A part of Strang Communications Company
600 Rinehart Road
Lake Mary, Florida 32746
www.creationhouse.com

*This book is dedicated
to my second son, Joshua,
whose tender spirit refreshes my soul.
You have nothing to prove
and even less to earn.*

Acknowledgments

If no man is an island unto himself, then no writer can ever know and reveal his own soul without the love and affirmation of others. Many wonderful people have supported my vision during the process of writing this book.

To my wife, Judith, my confederate in redigging old wells and revealing new paths, thank you for seeing my potential long before I had the courage to believe in myself.

To the members of Christ the King CitiChurch, thank you for allowing me the freedom to grow as a leader. Many of the principles contained in this book were birthed out of our quest to "grow up into Christ in all things." The decade we spent together forged my character in a significant and lasting way.

To those who initiated and assisted in the development of this project: Alyse Lounsberry for barging into my life and wrecking my schedule, Tom Freiling for inspiring me to put pen to paper, Sonja Brown for your insight into chapter nine and Bridget Jentzsch for your eagle eyes in proofreading. Thank you, Barbara Dycus, for your encouragement, affirmation and keen editorial insight.

To those spiritual leaders who have shaped my life through writing, teaching, preaching and reaching. You know who you are.

Contents

Foreword

I HAVE BEEN PRIVILEGED to nuture, feed and direct some of the Lord's sheep and lambs under His direct super-vision. Often in my involvement in the "people-helping" business, I have had to come alongside them in the power of the Holy Spirit and act as a "midwife" in the birth process of their experience of their unique and true worth in Christ. In recent years I have come to feel a great deal of empathy with them in the light of my own struggles and challenges as it relates to celebrating whom God has made us to be. I have come to believe that as spiritual friends of the Bridegroom we are to bring His loving and healing presence into their existence at a deeper and more profound level. Often I find that their misbelief and their limited belief is at the root of their emotional pain. Helping them recognize their inadequate mental models and encouraging them in the process of the renewing of their minds take a great deal of time, patience and process.

My trusted friend Terry Crist has given us some of the tools that invite us to reconsider the mental models we unconsciously embrace that rob us of the truth that sets us free. It seems as though he is inviting us to repent of far more than our inadequate performance in the area of pleasing God. His invitation is that we "dump our files" of our inaccurate and inadequate beliefs about who we think we are and embrace by faith whom God truly calls us to be and become. There is a great deal to contemplate and consider in this millennial apologetic on the "new man." Whether your personal study on the new creation has ever led you this far or not, one thing is for certain: *The Image Maker* will cause you to take a fresh look at one of the great truths of your redemption in Christ and to celebrate your true value as a child of the Father.

One poignant moment in *The Image Maker* that gripped my heart is the story of Terry's personal encounter in the dentist office with an out-of-touch and incongruent father and his precious daughter suffering from Down's syndrome. I was reminded of our considerable need for agents of healing in society. May you find great encouragment and a rich resource of the Spirit of life in Christ Jesus as you peruse the pages of this thorough and well-done treatise.

—Dr. Mark Chironna
The Master's Touch International Church
Orlando, Florida

Introduction

THE SEARCH FOR self-esteem has rapidly become the Holy Grail of the twenty-first century. In the quest to discover our inherent worth, many Christians have become vulnerable to the ancient enemies of humanism and pantheism. This battle is not just being waged in the New Age community any longer; it has invaded the church through a subtle distortion of the biblical principles of "identity, image and design."

Because of society's desire to fill the self-esteem void, approbation-peddling capitalists have flooded the market.

Just turn on late-night television, and it won't be long before an infomercial magically appears promising far more than mere mortals can ever possibly deliver. If you're a housewife experiencing low self-esteem because your friends are all living the high life without cutting coupons or changing diapers, you can get your esteem lifted faster than they can get their faces lifted. Pastors struggling to offer as much fanfare as the "competition" around the corner can find self-fulfillment in believing that "we may be small, but we are pure." Struggling salesmen are the perfect targets for these "esteem builders"—just slightly longer than it takes to loosen that sweaty collar, you can think like a winner and discover how to rebuff personal rejection. One writer calls this motivational pabulum the "twelve-step program for the terminally modest."

Prior to our recent culture shift toward post-modernism, most Americans used to ask themselves, "Is this the right thing to do?", before making any decision with the capacity to impact their lives, communities or nation. We were accustomed to considering the long-term consequences of our actions. Now, rather than taking into account the ramifications of our personal choices, most people simply ask the question, "How will this make me *feel?*" We are living in a national culture that has chosen to esteem *personal feelings* over *moral choices.*

Many contemporary self-help gurus suggest that the reason people are so defeated in life is simply because they "don't feel good about themselves." The apparent mission of the self-esteem "movement" is to deceive you into believing that self-esteem is essential for your psychological well-being. As you will discover in this book, I intend to address this issue directly, because there is a vast difference between the concept of self-esteem and the truth concerning our individual self-worth. Neither term is in the Bible; therefore we need to compare a number of secular definitions with their scriptural counterparts.

Let's begin by contrasting the principles of self-esteem with the biblical concept of self-worth. William James, considered by many to be the father of American psychology, defined self-esteem this way: Self-esteem = $\frac{success}{pretentions}$.[1] Based upon that definition, your self-esteem is a reflection of how you are performing (your successes) compared to how you think you should be performing (your pretensions). If you accept this definition, your self-esteem should fluctuate each day based upon your actions in life. Furthermore, basing self-esteem upon personal performance may cause you to seek the approval of man at the expense of God's will for your life.

Self-worth, on the other hand, is an entirely different matter. Our value as human beings is not based upon any of our personal abilities. It is predicated upon one simple fact: The infinite Creator of the universe created us in His personal image. Because of that, man's basic worth never fluctuates because it is secure in the identity of The Image Maker—not the image bearer. So, while your self-esteem goes up and down, your essential worth and value are forever stable. Even though you may *feel* worthless at times and extremely worthwhile at other times, those feelings don't change the fact that The Image Maker considers you "fearfully and wonderfully" made. Self-esteem is based upon what you feel, but self-worth is based upon who you are.

Another way of contrasting these two opposing paradigms is to say that self-esteem is based upon performance, but self-worth is based upon an understanding of your identity. That understanding can be regained only through a personal relationship with The Image Maker. As you will discover through these writings, all men bear the basic components of the Creator's personal image, even though

3

the internal dimension of man is moving in the opposite direction of his eternal purpose prior to spiritual rebirth. With the formation of the new creation, we are brought back into harmony (spirit, soul and body) and into the image and likeness of almighty God.

If you wonder why we have become a nation of increasing addictions and accelerating dependencies, it is because society is attempting to blot out the pain that comes when people have lost their identity. Men and women fall into the addictions of food, alcohol and prescription drugs while desperately trying to find significance, worth and value. Our children roam the streets in gangs in their search for acceptance. Our teenage daughters become pregnant in their quest for worth and value. The enemy is systematically dismantling this nation through the spirit of rejection and the lack of worth and value, which only come with the ignorance of one's essential identity.

In a desperate attempt to satisfy the longing, we try to fill the void with materialism, sexual gratification, achievement, self-improvement—even religion. But none seem to work, because this is a spiritual problem, and a spiritual problem cannot be met with natural solutions. A spiritual question cannot be answered with a natural response.

Helen Keller was struck deaf, dumb and mute by a virus at the age of nineteen months. Trapped in a world without words, colors or music, she was locked in the loneliness of an isolated existence until her perseverant teacher, Annie Sullivan, broke into her silence with one single word—*water*. When Helen discovered that one word, she discovered the world. One word became the doorway to the future and the breakthrough of one of the most admirable people who ever lived.

My prayer is that somewhere in the pages of this book you will discover one word that will irrevocably change your future. It may be one of these words: *identity, incarnation, redemption* or *righteousness.* Your supernatural key to transformation may be any one of ten thousand other words that open the door of kingdom life to you. Discover it...believe it...meditate upon it...and demonstrate it!

PART I:
DESIGNED AND DEFINED

This generation will never
settle the mystery of God as long
as we ignore the mystery of man.

One

HOW IN THE WORLD
DID WE GET HERE?

If I could tell the world just one thing,
It would be that we're all OK
And not to worry 'cause worry is wasteful
And useless in times like these.
I won't be made useless;
I won't be idle with despair.
I will gather myself around my faith
For light does the darkness most fear.[1]

—JEWEL KILCHER

W E SHOULD HAVE seen it coming. The warning signs were there from the beginning. Though they had been carefully masked, all the symptoms of a terminal generation had advanced to the point of critical mass. When the incubation period was finally matured, the virus exploded, carrying its deadly effects from Arkansas to Kentucky, before moving on to Oregon, Colorado, Georgia and who knows where next.

When did it begin? How did we fall so fast and so far from grace? When did drug abuse, physical assault,

9

robbery and murder replace talking in class, chewing gum and running in the hall as the major policy violations in American public schools?

I cannot remember being as significantly affected by any national tragedy as I was by the Littleton, Colorado, high school shootings that abruptly aborted the lives of thirteen promising young men and women, including the school's athletics coach. As a nation groaned in pain and cultural analysts questioned "Why?", the truth seemed so obvious. It was as obvious as the vacant wall in the Columbine High School foyer, which should have held the Ten Commandments. It was as obvious as the full-color evolution chart hanging on the walls of the biology classroom. It was as obvious as our failure to discern the murderous hatred in the eyes of Eric Harris and Dylan Klebold.

For weeks following the senseless slaughter, the question "Why?" was on the lips of almost everyone in our nation. National magazines and local newspapers clamored for a motive.[2] Cultural analysts dissected every imaginable motive, but the answer was not forthcoming. Perhaps the more important question to be asked was not one that we were willing to entertain. Rather than asking "Why?" during the months following the tragedy, I found myself considering the question "Why not?" After all, what else can we expect from teenagers who have been told that ideas and actions are without consequences and that we are just occupying one empty moment on the evolutionary road to nowhere? The feeling of hopelessness contained within the heart of this generation was recently summarized in the lyrics of a popular song written by a young artist. "I belong to the Blank Generation. I have no beliefs. I belong to no community, tradition or anything like that. I'm lost in this vast, vast world. I belong nowhere. I have absolutely no identity."[3] We have sown to the wind, and we are reaping the whirlwind.

How in the World Did We Get Here?

THE LONG ROAD TO NOWHERE

AT THE CLOSE of the nineteenth century, both Christians and non-Christians in Western culture agreed about most of the essential issues of life. Almost everyone believed that God existed, had created the world and had established a certain value system, which was reflected in the Bible. Society as a whole reflected a unified worldview. Even those who were not professing Christians basically agreed with the need for moral standards in society. But a century ago that common consent began to unravel, and it has been deteriorating substantially with every decade since.

There were three philosophical theories that began to destroy this harmony. First, Charles Darwin and other scientists challenged the biblical model of creation. As a result of that dispute, believers and unbelievers alike began to debate the validity of creational science. Scientists then began to declare that people were simply the product of chance and natural selection. For the first time in Western society, the identity of man was under question.

Once science had opened the door to basic humanism, philosophers began to debate the purpose of our existence. Based upon a logical assumption, they deduced that if we were not here because a loving God created us in His image, then personal destiny was a concept to be rejected. Suddenly, men and women began to question their purpose in life. This second assumption opened the floodgates for disillusionment and despair in our culture.

History shows us the ongoing quest throughout the ages to know and fully understand the origin, purpose and destiny of man. In one of his discourses, the philosopher Plato describes his teacher Socrates as a man fixated on one primary objective in life—to know and understand himself. This fixation is reflective of the burning passion that fuels

11

the philosophical search. All men either consciously or subconsciously have one supreme desire deep within their being—to know and understand "Who am I?" That question cannot be answered apart from a biblical understanding of the original image and ultimate purpose of man. The answer is found in the inceptive design of man by The Image Maker.

Personal destiny is the result of divine design. We cannot possibly hope to know the answer to "Why am I here?" apart from an understanding of "Who am I?" The comprehension of one's identity serves as the foundation for the revelation of one's purpose. This revelation fuels the fire of exploration as we seek to understand our personal mission in life.

In his insightful book *Burden of Truth*, Chuck Colson observes:

> Philosophy professor Lowell Nissen, writing in a journal called *Studies in the History and Philosophy of Science*, says biology cannot get rid of the language of purpose... There is simply no way to get rid of purpose in biology. It would be a lot smarter to get rid of the dogma of naturalism. If we accept that God designed the world, then the language of purpose makes perfect sense. Eyes were made for seeing—made by God. As Christians, we should be eager to talk about divine purpose in the world. The fact that biology cannot get along without the notion is a great argument we can use with our skeptical friends.[4]

Finally, as people questioned their origin and purpose, the third presupposition widened the philosophical gap even further. If the God of the Bible did not exist, then the moral standards of the Bible should be rejected as well. These issues have developed for decades, until by now most people are convinced that absolute truth (including moral truth) does not exist. Moral absolutes have been replaced by ethical relativism.

The invasion of Eastern mysticism in the 1960s enhanced Darwin's theory of evolution by making the Bible appear as just another religious alternative, confusing countless thousands. Questions of purpose and existence caused many to turn to drugs and Eastern spiritualism. The concepts of reincarnation swept through a spiritually hungry populace, giving rise to hundreds of new cults. Not everyone shaved their head or embraced communal living. But for those who actually adopted Eastern philosophy when the University of California at Berkeley opened its Western doors, life wasn't proving to be worth the anguished price that they were paying to live it. If the best one's New Age karma cycle could offer in the next life was a goose or a moose, then pass the drugs. And if the random existence evolution coincidentally handed us was only about barely surviving, life had become abysmally cheap. The most apparent result of this downward trend in contemporary society is the identity crisis that exists within the soul of this generation.

SEARCHING FOR AN IDENTITY

THE GROUNDWORK OF this moral revolution was laid when scientists began to question the origin of man. As Anthony Hoekema, former professor of systematic theology at Calvin Theological Seminary, sagely writes:

> The question of man has therefore become one of the most crucial problems of our day. Philosophers are wrestling with it; sociologists are trying to answer it; psychologists and psychiatrists are facing it; ethicists and social activists are attempting to solve it. Novelists

and dramatists also concern themselves with this question. Dostoyevski's penetrating novels are attempts to answer it, along with the related question, "Why is man here?" Jean-Paul Sarte and Albert Camus have tried to give us their non-Christian answers to the question, whereas writers like Graham Greene and Morris West have tried to give us their Christian answers. Virtually every contemporary novel or play deals with the question, "What is man?"[5]

I am convinced that this generation will never settle the mystery of God as long as we ignore the mystery of man. To paraphrase 1 John 4:20, "If you fail to identify your brother whom you have seen, how can you identify God whom you have not seen?" It is our blindness to the basic worth of mankind that prevents us from even acknowledging the existence of God. To devalue the creation is to deny the Creator. To devalue the identity of the image bearer is to deny the creatorial right of The Image Maker.

- When we refuse to acknowledge who we are as image bearers of the Omnipotent One, we deny our right to dominion and authority.

- When we refuse to acknowledge who we are as image bearers of the Omniscient One, we deny our right to know the truth.

- When we refuse to acknowledge who we are as image bearers of the Omnipresent One, we deny our right to live in His presence.

LIFE WITHOUT MEANING

WITHOUT FALLING INTO the subtle snares of humanism, the fundamental importance of the identity of man cannot be overemphasized. While I was ministering recently in Buffalo, New York, Pastor Tommy Reid graciously took me on a personal tour of the century-old Roycroft Campus, the "utopian craft community" of Elbert Hubbard, one of America's most influential humanists. Through his monthly periodical, *The Philistine*, Hubbard propagated the doctrine of man while ridiculing those who believed in the personal existence of God. He went as far as to rewrite the Apostles' Creed, changing the verbiage and substituting the word "man" for "God." His chief aim was to establish the worth of man apart from the existence of God.

While walking the red brick pathway under the canopy of beautiful old oak trees, I was struck by the sense of hopelessness that permeated the atmosphere. Even though the Roycroft Campus was brightly decorated with positive statements espousing the sovereignty of man and the possibilities of the future, a damp darkness seemed to saturate everything in view. In spite of the physical beauty around me, I could not shake the feeling that this was a morally bankrupt community. Although Hubbard would have denied this fact, his was a fatalistic approach to life. His attempt to bolster the self-esteem of man by denying the existence of God failed miserably. While encouraging human achievement, humanism leaves man with no future beyond the grave. How difficult it must be to search for one's personal purpose in life while denying the principle of divine design.

As we work our way through this book, it is important for us to make a sharp distinction between a humanistic study of man vs. a scriptural study of man. Furthermore, we will also need to define the significant difference between *fallen man*, who distorted the likeness of God, and *redeemed man*, who has been restored back to the full potential of the original design. At this point in our journey, let us simply establish the fact that the understanding of man as a created being in the image of God is both significant and relevant. The creation of man provides a physical and material expression of the identity of The Image Maker.

"WHAT IS MAN THAT THOU ART MINDFUL OF HIM?"

CREATION SERVES AS a material confirmation to the existence of God. Romans 1 declares, "Since the creation of the world His invisible attributes are clearly seen, being understood by the things that are made, even His eternal power and Godhead, so that they [mankind] are without excuse" (Rom. 1:20). As an "extreme" sports fanatic, I have been privileged to explore many regions of the earth. When standing on the top of a rugged mountain peak viewing uninhabited valleys below, lying in a sleeping bag staring up at the Northern Lights displaying the celestial wonders of the heavens or watching the Southern Cross from the jungles of central Africa, I am compelled by the evidence to acknowledge the existence of God. But none of these natural wonders testify of sovereign deity any greater than the mystery of man. No wonder mankind has been under attack from the beginning.

Over fifteen centuries ago Saint Augustine, bishop of Hippo, condemned the fact that "men go forth to wonder at the heights of the mountains, the huge waves of sea, the broad flow of rivers, at the vast compass of the ocean, the courses of the stars; and they pass by themselves without wondering."

Consider for a moment the wonder of the human frame. The psalmist David poetically described man as being "fearfully and wonderfully made" (Ps. 139:14). With the birth of our first son, Judith and I sat quietly for hours counting and recounting fragile fingers and tiny toes. Strangely enough, of all the wonders contained in this bundle of joy, I was intrigued the most with the delicate little fingernails replicating my own. That initial astonishment did not lessen with the birth of our second son, and finally the third. Born to a brown-haired father and a blond mother, we produced one redhead, one blond and one with dark brown hair!

There is no scientific achievement by man that even compares to the creation of man. We were created as the crowning achievement of all creation. I am constantly amazed at the complexity of the human design.

Consider this. A single cell of the human body contains as much information as ninety volumes of the *Encyclopedia Britannica*, and yet five million red blood cells and five million white blood cells would fit on the head of a straight pin. Some cells are programmed to manufacture and maintain the material that forms bone and cartilage. Others form skin, muscles and internal organs.

The structure of the human body is composed of DNA, which consists of an estimated three billion pairs of nucleotides, called base pairs, arranged like the steps of a twisting ladder. Along the helical ladder, these pairs occur in a pattern otherwise known as a sequence. They are marked off by clusters of hundreds of thousands—in some cases millions—of base pairs, which constitute genes. Geneticists have determined that each cell contains a maximum of one hundred thousand genes. DNA is so finely constructed and compressed that all of the cells contained within a human body could fit into a half-inch square cube; yet if the DNA were joined together end to end, the strand would stretch around the earth more than three million times.

A single human neuron has limited capabilities, but if you place ten billion neurons with sixty trillion synapses together in the cerebral cortex, then an individual will have a brain that thinks and directs neurological signals to the entire human body.

As playwright Tom Stoppard once described it, "The

idea of God is slightly more plausible than the alternative proposition that, given enough time, some green slime could write Shakespeare's sonnets."[6] The formation of man was no random accident.

Without the theory of evolution, the secular humanist would have to rely on The Image Maker as the source of all life, which would therefore destroy his philosophical framework for humanism. As a matter of fact, without the theory of evolution there is no logical basis for secular humanism. Humanism is based upon the flawed presupposition that approximately four billion years ago the first particle of life was spontaneously generated by an accidental combination of chemicals and energy. Eventually this particle reproduced itself and began the process of improving and reproducing until it finally evolved into mankind. George Gaylord Simpson, a leading proponent of evolution, once wrote, "Man is the result of a purposeless and natural process that did not have him in mind. He was not planned. He is a state of matter, a form of life, a sort of animal, and a species of the Order Primates, akin nearly or remotely to all of life and indeed to all that is material."[7] Those who hold to this position see man as nothing more than a cosmic accident.

The humanistic aim is to rid society of the presence of the Creator by denying the existence of man in His image. No humanist has been heard any louder in this generation than Charles Darwin. Darwin vociferously engaged in a crusade to eradicate the existence of God from the minds of men by scientifically challenging the concepts of design and purpose. His ideas later formed the basis of thought for John Dewey, who in turn had a profound influence on the development of our educational system.

EVOLUTION PRODUCES REVOLUTION

WHERE DARWINISM HAS ruled as the predominant worldview,

violence has prevailed. The Franco-Prussian War of 1870 set the philosophical course for literally hundreds of subsequent conflicts by using Darwin's theory as the basis for militant oppression. In more recent times, China, Russia and Nazi Germany provide documentation for the abuse of human rights based upon their antitheistic worldview. Even the demonized drive toward "ethnic cleansing" in Eastern Europe has its roots in the soil of natural selection.

Karl Marx was proud to acknowledge Charles Darwin's theory as the scientific basis for his views on class struggle. It is said that Marx even considered dedicating his book *Das Kapital* to Darwin. Marxism was once defined as "Darwinism applied to human society."[8] One need not look far in history to discover the connection between evolution and revolution. Joseph Stalin boastfully declared that "evolution prepares for revolution and creates the ground for it. Revolution consummates the process of evolution and facilitates its further activity."[9] Evolution lays the groundwork for social savagery.

When a man believes in punctuated evolution, that he is nothing more than an evolved animal, he subconsciously settles for life at its lowest common denominator. (The natural instinct to survive and procreate is endemic to wild animals.) And when man embraces the concept of spontaneous generation, that he is nothing more than the product of colliding dust particles, it is no wonder he struggles with a lack of worth and value. But when man believes in special creation—that he is the product of divine design, created by The Image Maker, then that man will rise to discover his personal destiny in life.

Have you ever considered the social ramifications of Darwin's theory of evolution? Charles Darwin's 1859 book, *The Origin of the Species*, was subtitled *The Preservation of Favored Races in the Struggle for Life*. So perverted were his views on the purpose of man that Darwin openly taught that all whites would eventually kill all blacks—as well as the other "lower races"—within a century or two, and that it would merely be ongoing evolutionary development in progress. Adolph Hitler's most notorious work, *Mein Kampf* (*My Struggle*), was based upon evolutionary theory. He publicly aligned himself with Darwin, identifying him as a prophet with special insight into the history of man and the future of the species.

When the belief that God created the heavens and the earth is rejected (as it is in our day), basic human rights are reinterpreted and, in some cases, even exterminated. The Declaration of Independence bases its doctrine of "unalienable rights" upon the doctrine of creation. The Declaration of Independence states, "Men are endowed by their Creator with certain unalienable rights, that among these are life, liberty and the pursuit of happiness."

When you remove the presence of the Creator, you then remove the basis for "unalienable rights." No Creator equals no "unalienable human rights." That's why racism is not just a sin against humanity, but it is ultimately a sin against The Image Maker. Racism spurns the creative handiwork of a sovereign God who created all men in His image and likeness. As a matter of fact, the very word *human* means "shaded or colored man." Black, brown, peach, white, red and yellow, we each reflect another dimension of His divine image. But more importantly, more fundamentally, John 4:24 declares that God is Spirit. Regardless of color or shade or skin texture, all men are created in the image of the Creator who is Spirit. We are spirit beings confined to a human experience for this moment of time.

ENLIGHTENING A GENERATION

WHAT A DIFFERENCE Adam's created heritage produces in

20

the psyche of man over the dog-eat-dog stigma of human-istic thinking. When we come to believe that we have been carefully constructed in the likeness and image of a per-sonal being, even apart from the spiritual issues, the consti-tution of natural life has great value and sacred implica-tions. Life is The Image Maker's engendered essence, so it is not biologically inferior. Human life contains unmatched value in the created order of all life forms. What sets man, the image bearer, apart from the rest of creation is the pur-pose of his original design.

We are told by cosmic humanists (the New Age world-view) that all life has equal value. According to Ingrid Newkirk, president of People for the Ethical Treatment of Animals, "A rat is a pig is a dog is a boy."[10] I have often won-dered what psychological effect this must have on the child who believes that his life is the equivalent of ham and eggs. And furthermore, what registers in the heart of this genera-tion when many of the same people protesting to save the whales also protect the right to murder unborn babies?

Just one generation after moral relativism became the standard of our nation, most image bearers cannot dis-tinguish between "normal" and "abnormal" or even "sub-normal." The standard by which man is to be judged has been rejected, leaving us without the ability to judge what is acceptable to God. Like Israel during the period of the judges, every man does that which is right in his *own* eyes.

We are sending mixed signals to this generation. We cannot have it both ways. The principles of evolution and special creation are philosophically opposed to one another. They will not coexist. As long as we sow the seeds of worthlessness in this generation, we will reap the fruit of destruction. No one, in my estimation, says this better than the brilliant Christian apologist, Ravi Zacharias, who recently wrote, "We have given our children contradictory

21

assumptions about life and then are shocked at their evil behavior and the disintegration of their lives."[11] The Scriptures clearly state, "If the trumpet makes an uncertain sound, who will prepare for battle?" (1 Cor. 14:8).

Ironically, in a politically correct, religiously tolerant, multicultural society, we still subtly reinforce the principles of male chauvinism, class segregation and racial oppression because of the underpinnings of evolution in our educational system. While paying lip service to the principles of tolerance and diversity, our public schools continue to teach the amoral values of natural selection. Illustrated in our textbooks, portrayed in our motion pictures, brought to life in our video games, evolutionary theory continues to shape the collective conscience of our nation. When the head is sick, the whole body becomes defiled.

Society is searching for peace while continuing to reject the presence of the Prince of Peace—not realizing that Christianity is the only true basis for tolerance and diversity. Only as we live the life of Christ before a broken and hurting world will society discover grace and peace. Those cultures that function according to the principles of divine design are destined to discover true worth and value.

While recently ministering to a young man struggling with his purpose in life, I heard the Holy Spirit speak words that shocked my mind and broke my heart. He said, "This young man cannot see his purpose because he has never embraced his worth." And in that moment, I suddenly realized that the young man sitting before me was one of the fortunate ones who had escaped the abortion mills of his generation. While thirty million of his peers were callously slaughtered around him, he escaped with life, but without a sense of self-worth. Adding to his sense of inadequacy, sociologists further devalued his generation by using a symbol of hopelessness for their identification rather than a name.

How in the World Did We Get Here?

We cannot systematically debase a generation through distorted instructions and still expect them to have a healthy view of the worth of man. What we devalue in the classroom we destroy in the streets. As we dispose of our unwanted fetuses, we bury our young in increasing numbers. The cries of pain in the offices of the abortion clinics are muffled by the sounds of gunfire in our streets. To the calloused humanist, this may simply be the modern urban equivalent of the "survival of the fittest." As acclaimed author Philip Yancey once stated, "Either individual human beings have inherent worth, bestowed by a Creator, or we are mere animals subject only to the laws we forcibly impose upon one another."[12]

On the fateful morning following the Columbine High School massacre, I boarded a plane on my way to minister in another city. As tears ran down my cheeks, the bold headline screamed from the paper lying on my lap, *"Our Kids Are Crying Bullets."* Sorry, Jewel, we're not OK.

The divine design made
provision for your complete and
ultimate success in life, but you have
to believe it, receive it and practice it.

Two

Discovering the

Divine Design

Our deepest fear is not that we are inadequate. Our deepest
fear is that we are powerful beyond measure. It is our light, not
our darkness, that most frightens us. We ask ourselves, "Who am I to
be brilliant, gorgeous, talented and fabulous?" Actually who are you
not to be? You are a child of God. Your playing small does not serve
the world. There is nothing enlightening about shrinking so that other
people won't feel insecure around you. We are born to make manifest
the glory of God that is within us. It is not just in some of us; it is in
everyone. And as we let our light shine, we unconsciously give
other people permission to do the same. As we are liberated
from our own fear, our presence automatically liberates others.
—Nelson Mandela, 1994 Inaugural Speech

WHEN NELSON MANDELA spoke these words in his
inaugural speech on that historic day in the
Republic of South Africa, he was addressing a nation that
had been subjected to apartheid for half a century. In this
remarkable nation teeming with beauty and potential, the
black African had been subjected to indescribable acts of
cruelty. Apartheid had empowered a small minority of the
population with the freedom to prosper while the remaining 90 percent were treated as worthless chattel
without basic human rights.

The struggle over apartheid in South Africa was a microcosm of the conflict found in the human race, in every nation, in each generation. As long as men deny the principles of the divine intent in the creation of man, each generation moves one step further away from the power of significance and self-worth.

Human rights, whether they are granted or not, are endemic to the essential identity carefully formed in every human being. The rights to think and act freely are an integral part of the divine design of mankind. And in South Africa, as in our own nation, the rights of men were not being usurped in an antitheistic state, but rather one that considered itself Christian. Tragically, racial oppression was primarily supported by misguided fundamentalists who refused to acknowledge the universal nature of the image bearer.

BACK TO BASICS

AT A TIME when scientific research has not only decoded many of the biological mysteries of life but has also begun to experiment with ways of significantly altering it, you might ask what benefit can come from an Old Testament study of the origin of man. How can a collection of sacred texts written almost three thousand years ago by a culturally confined people with a prescientific worldview have any influence on our search for the purpose and meaning of life?

The answer to that question is determined by your view of the Old Testament. Those who see it as an outdated manuscript that only reflects the thinking of its ancient writers will devalue its significance in defining life in the twenty-first century. However, those committed to the timelessness of the Scripture along with its ongoing relevance as a pattern for living, must inquire of it to determine if it has anything at all to say to the existential crisis that challenges modern man.

Discovering the Divine Design

If the Old Testament has any relevance to modern man, it is to address questions of divine design and ultimate destiny, the same concerns that are found deep within the heart of the New Testament. My purpose is to begin here by examining the foundation of the Scriptures to discover what they have to say about the purpose and destiny of man.

ORIGINATION DETERMINES DESTINATION

"ALL HISTORY, ONCE you strip the rind off the kernel, is really spiritual," wrote historian Arnold Toynbee.[1] That's why I believe the creational record speaks far more of the nature and character of God than it does of the nature of rocks, trees and animals. It is in the creation record that The Image Maker exercises His first opportunity to step out of eternity and into time. And He takes advantage of this inaugural moment to reveal some fundamental principles concerning His nature. First impressions are lasting.

The Book of Genesis is the seedbed for everything God has done throughout the history of man. When you truly discover what God initiated in the beginning, then you will understand what He is presently doing today. God's purposes have never changed! The Image Maker is still working from the same blueprint that He began with in the Garden of Eden at the genesis of earth life.

Beginnings determine endings. This is the reason why contemporary man desires nothing any greater than new beginnings. We find ourselves in the most painful moments of life, wishing we would have acted differently when faced with previous challenges. In the wake of a broken marriage, a failed business or a fragmented family, we long for the opportunity to begin again.

Several years ago when my children were just beginning the "Nintendo experience," I recall hearing them occasionally shout, "Do over!" Finally, curiosity got the best of me. I crept over to the door of their bedroom and cracked it just enough to see clearly inside. I watched in silent humor as they played their way into a difficult situation from which they could not recover, only to shout "Do over!" before hitting the reset button.

But life doesn't have a reset button. That's why Scripture declares that God's mercies "are new every morning" (Lam. 3:23). With the dawning of each new day, The Image Maker offers us the opportunity to forget the past and begin again.

Throughout the years I have met those Christians who live with the idea that God's original purpose failed when Adam sinned and that God has been living in a "damage control" mode ever since. Nothing could be further from the truth. Aside from being ridiculous, this philosophy is dangerous to believe because it subtly implies that The Image Maker is not to be trusted. After all, if He failed with Adam, He could fail with us. So rather than trusting in God's sovereign ability to care for them, some people live with a tormenting sense of insecurity. But when you understand that God genuinely saw the end from the beginning, that Adam's sin did not catch Him by surprise and that in spite of the failures of men He has remained unequivocally faithful to His original design for the earth, then you can live life in great peace and security!

God's ways are not only perfect, but they are also perfectly consistent. Just as He has never deviated from His divine design, He has also never forsaken His original mission as it is revealed in the record of creation. Malachi 3:6 states, "I am the LORD, I do not change." This refers not only to His immutable character, but also to His original purpose and design for man. There is great importance to this simple truth, because once you understand the pattern with which He works, you will then discover the present application. What God began at the genesis of earth life is still being carried out today through the power of the Holy Spirit under the administration of King Jesus.

THE MASTER ARCHITECT

MYLES MUNROE HAS eloquently stated:

> You will never discover who you were meant to be if you use another person to find yourself. You will never know what you can do by using what I've done to measure your ability. You will never know why you exist if you use my existence to measure it. All you will see is what I've done or who I am. If you want to know who you are, look at God. The key to understanding life is in the source of life, not in the life itself. You are who you are because God took you out of Himself. If you want to know who you are, you must look at the Creator, not the creation.[2]

My purpose is sharing this information with you is to empower you to rise to a new level of living. The divine design made provision for your complete and ultimate success in life, but you have to believe it, receive it and practice it. And that journey begins by discovering the wealth of potential that was programmed into God's original intention for man.

> Then God said, "Let us make humankind in our image, according to our likeness; and let them have dominion over the fish of the sea, and over the birds of the air, and over the cattle, and over all the wild animals of the earth, and over every creeping thing that creeps upon the earth." So God created humankind in his image, in the image of God he created them; male and female he created them. God blessed them, and God said to them, "Be fruitful and multiply, and fill

the earth and subdue it; and have dominion over the fish of the sea and over the birds of the air and over every living thing that moves upon the earth."

—GENESIS 1:26–28, RSV

The primary thought that impresses me as I carefully consider the language of Genesis 1 is that man was created in the image and likeness of God. The word translated as "image" is *tselem;* the word translated as "likeness" is *demuth.* In the Hebrew language there is no conjunction between the two expressions; the text simply states, "let us make man in our image, after our likeness." The Septuagint and the Vulgate, however, insert the word *and* between the two words, leaving us with the impression that "image" and "likeness" refer to two different things. My personal belief is that even though these two words appear to be synonyms, there are some subtle, but significant differences between them.

If there is one thing I have learned from a lifetime of Bible study, it is that God is not redundant. He does not stutter. When He repeats Himself in the course of Scripture, the "law of repetition" is for the purpose of further expansion. I am convinced that God intended for us to picture man formed in both the likeness *and* the image of God.

Although the words *image* and *likeness* are occasionally used interchangeably, when used together they reveal a broader picture of the original design of man. This view has been commonly accepted throughout church history, beginning with Irenaeus, bishop of Lyons, in the second century. In his mission to refute the doctrinal heresy of Gnosticism, Irenaeus taught that God originally created man in His image *and* after His likeness. He believed that man's likeness to God, however, was lost in the Fall, whereas the image of God continued to be revealed through the whole of mankind. Only through the process of redemption

30

could the likeness of God be restored to man.

Listen as Irenaeus describes it in his own words:

> But if the Spirit be wanting to the soul, he who is such is indeed of an animal nature, and being left carnal, shall be an imperfect being, possessing indeed the image in his formation, but not receiving the similitude through the Spirit, and thus is this being imperfect.[3]

Through years of personal study, I have developed the conviction that this is the appropriate position on the matter. As you will discover in the next chapter, fallen man still possesses the image of God, but he desperately needs the atoning work of Redemption to restore him back to the likeness of God that he expressed before the Fall. This distinction enables me to see the basic worth of all men while also recognizing the special nature of redeemed man. Through the power of the new birth experience, Jesus Christ restores the *likeness* of God the Father back to fallen man.

The Hebrew word for "image," *tselem*, is derived from a root word that means "to carve" or "to cut." Strong's concordance defines *tselem* as "a representative figure, especially an idol." It implies the visual image of a carved likeness of an animal or a person. We find this word consistently used in the Old Testament in reference to idols and other representations, usually of pagan deities. This same word is found in Exodus 20 where the second of the Ten Commandments forbids the construction of any "graven image." When applied to the creation of man in Genesis 1, the word *tselem* indicates that man "images" God; that is, he is a visual representation of God.

THE FACE OF GRACE

THE NEW TESTAMENT reveals a similar picture when describing the Man Christ Jesus. Hebrews 1:3 declares,

"The Son is the radiance of God's glory and the exact representation of his being" (NIV). The glory that Christ the Son radiates is not His own but is the glory of God the Father. The Greek word translated here as "exact representation" (*charakter*) is an enlightening one. According to W. E. Vine, it describes a "a stamp or impress, as on a coin or a seal, in which case the seal or die which makes an impression bears the image produced by it, and, vice versa, all the features of the image correspond respectively with those of the instrument producing it."[4] We discover in this word the picture of a reigning monarch who sends a royal decree into the far corners of his domain. After preparing his message, his final act is to fold the paper, drop hot wax on the edge and firmly press his ring into the wax as a seal of his authority. After drawing back his hand, he leaves behind an exact representation of his signet of authority.

The first Adam was the premier representation of his Father. The last Adam was the perfect representation of His Father. It is difficult to impress the point any greater. Man was not just created in the image of God in some generic abstract way. He was the earth-bound representation of God in every trait. Every quality, every characteristic, every attribute that was present in The Image Maker was formed in the life of the image bearer.

There are three dimensions to the Hebrew word *likeness*. According to W. E. Vine, the word for "likeness," *demut*, means "shape, figure, form or pattern." It was taken from a root word that means "to be like," "to resemble" or "to act like."[5] So we have the pattern, the image made according to the pattern and finally, the action of the image, which moves in accordance with its original design and purpose.

When used together, these two words, *image* and *likeness*, reveal man as an exact representation of God in both character and conduct. Interestingly, when God chose to project

32

Himself into this time-space world, He did so in the form of man, not in the form of a progressively developing ape with limited reasoning skills and an underdeveloped physiology.

This pattern man, Adam, was not a portentous brute dragging his long arms out of sixty billion years of primordial slime. He was formed as the image bearer of The Image Maker. The godless in previous generations embraced a deist concept of an unknowable creator because of the undeniable and logical order so evident in the earth. Plato called "him…it…" the "Prime Mover" and imagined this creator's earthly projections of "archtypical forms" as the substance visible on earth. Others have imagined God as some other impersonal being because the logic of His created order required a creative being. But God was expressing who He is in the creative language of a Father who was both personal and approachable.

ALIVE FOR THE VERY FIRST TIME

> And the LORD God formed man of the dust of the ground, and breathed into his nostrils the breath of life; and man became a living soul.
> —GENESIS 2:7, KJV

The Bible gives us a wonderfully tender, almost maternal picture of The Image Maker leaning over Adam as He breathes into him the breath of life. There is an endearing beauty in this scene as God imparts His being and very nature into the first man. As you read through the first two chapters of Genesis, you find that God spoke into existence everything Adam would be able to touch, smell, feel, hear and see. Yet when it came time to create mankind, The Image Maker lovingly handcrafted him. God did not speak Adam into existence through the power of His word. Neither did He send an angel to perform this sacred act. No, the Hebrew word *yatsar* implies that *El Ohim* (the Hebrew name that identifies Him as Creator) intimately formed and molded Adam as a potter forms a pot into shape. Both the Old Testament prophet Jeremiah and New Testament apostle Paul remind man in the Scriptures of his created heritage as clay on the Potter's wheel. (See Jeremiah 18:1–6; Romans 9:21.)

This intimate, creative act could not be more foreign to the concept of accidental evolution. The Father Himself kissed into Adam the breath of life, thereby giving him identity and purpose! If I close my eyes and meditate upon this scene long enough, I can almost see Adam lying there on the ground freshly formed by the creative hand of the infinite Architect of the universe. He is still damp from being sculpted out of the soil of Eden. I can picture the Father as He leaned over the clay form of Adam and breathed the breath of life into him. There is tender purpose in His movement. There is form to His divine image. The Scripture declares that God is Spirit, but in certain passages we are given glimpses of His anthropomorphic image. He has hands, eyes, ears, nostrils and a face. "For the eyes of the LORD are on the righteous, and His ears are open to their prayers; but the face of the LORD is against those who do evil" (1 Pet. 3:12).

Then the Father put His lips down on Adam and breathed into him His eternal superabundant life. The Hebrew word for this life is *chayim*, which is a plural word.[6] God breathed into Adam the breath of lives. This is not the beginning of "multiple lives" as the reincarnationist teaches, but rather the joining of Adam's spirit, soul and body into one functioning component. God supernaturally fused these three aspects of human life together to such a degree that the Word of God is the only power capable of distinguishing between them. (See Hebrews 4:12.) Suddenly the life of God's Spirit was infused into Adam's clay form with the life of his soul and body, integrating them into one singularly functioning unit. When Jesus came to restore Adam's spiritually dead descendants, He called it *zoe* life because of its full abundance in essence and meaning. As The Image Maker cradled the face of Adam in His hands, He looked into his eyes with a Father's pride and said, "This is My son. He looks just like Me. Not only is he created in My character, but he is also equipped to represent My conduct by managing the planet on My behalf."

I wonder what Adam's first thoughts were. He didn't progress in his being as we do today from infancy through stages of cognitive and spiritual development. When Adam was formed, he was suddenly brought to life with the full knowledge and revelation of God and His majestically created order. Suddenly, the smells, sights, tastes, textures and full glory of Adam's Creator were instantly before him. He was alive for the very first time.

Adam was created without any of the limitations with which we struggle. He was formed without any generational curse. There was no war within his members. Both his spirit and his flesh cried out in harmony for righteousness. He was created without any genetic flaw in his design. He did not have the crooked nose of a father or the cystic tissue of a mother. His brain was uncontaminated from negative thinking. His identity was undeniable, and his purpose was clear.

It is reported that Albert Einstein estimated that he used only one-third of the total capacity of his brain. If a man can suffer a two-thirds deficiency and still discover the law of relativity, what was Adam like? Without mental limitation, Adam gave names to each of the animals brought before him. While most men have an active vocabulary of four hundred words, Adam personally named thousands of animals in the Garden of Eden. I don't think we realize just how far man has fallen.

THE GENESIS OF SONSHIP

CAN YOU IMAGINE the Father's excitement as Adam opened his eyes for the very first time to the beauty and wonder of creation that was all around him? When Adam stood up from the dirt, he was not just in the image of God, but he was also in His likeness. The only way that I can even begin to relate this scene is to remember my initial reaction when my first son was born. Dripping wet, covered in mucus, head misshapen and screaming at the top of his lungs, he was the most beautiful human being on the face of the earth to me.

God is a father, and a father cannot be defined apart from his children. The sun, moon and stars defined Him as Creator. The earth and all of its glory defined Him as Supreme Architect. The angels in all of their glory defined Him as Ancient of Days. But it took Jesus to define Him as Father. It took Adam to acknowledge Him as Father. It takes you and me to receive Him as Father. And as a father, He has provided an inheritance for His children.

> So God created man in His own image; in the image of God He created him; male and female He created them. Then God blessed them, and God said to them, "Be fruitful and multiply; fill the earth and subdue it; have dominion over the fish of the sea, over the birds of the air, and over every living thing that moves on the earth."
>
> —GENESIS 1:27–28

The implementation of the divine intention found in this passage introduces a number of important advancements in defining humanity. The language of this verse reveals that mankind is not the end product of an evolutionary change but, in fact, is a brand-new idea, a being produced supernaturally out of nothing. Also, there is a twofold reminder that humans are the image of God: "So God created man in *His own image;* in *the image of God* He created him" (emphasis added). Even though this sentence is typical of Hebrew poetry, the repetition of the word *image* also has another purpose. The Scripture impresses upon us the fact that we are the very representatives of The Image Maker on earth!

What does it mean to be created in the image of God? I believe it is safe to assume that Adam shared in some of the characteristics of deity. As Herman Bavinck once stated, "Man does not simply *bear* or *have* the image of God; he *is* the image of God."[7] Even as the wayward sons of our heavenly Father, fallen man still shares in five characteristics of the original Adamic design. These attributes are:

- Man is a spirit being (Heb. 12:9).
- Man desires to interact with other spirit beings (Gen. 2:18; Ps. 63:1).
- Man has the capacity to reason intellectually (Isa. 29:24).
- Man has emotional qualities (Ps. 104:15; Rom. 9:2).
- Man was created with the right of free choice (1 Tim. 6:9; James 4:4).

COMMITTED TO THREE COVENANTS

IN ADDITION TO the description of man's creation, Genesis 1:26 contains the language of covenant. Long before the birth of Abraham, the first animal sacrifice and the revelation of covenant living, God created man in the spirit of covenant. This covenant, as with every subsequent covenant, contained an exchange of promise and responsibility. Man was created to live in covenant relationship in three dimensions: as a companion to God, in peace with other image bearers and as a steward of creation. I want to carefully examine these three covenants in order to discover the purpose of the creation of mankind.

Man was created to be in covenant with God. God created Adam to relate to His divine person individually, not institutionally. God never intended for Adam to interact with the Godhead abstractly, theologically or intellectually. Just as God is relational, in His image and after His likeness, so was Adam. This pattern man, in his state of sinless innocence, was not created as a servant; he was formed as a created son. Adam was designed to be a companion of God.

As the Father of light, The Image Maker cannot (by virtue of His own nature) fellowship with darkness. Therefore, it was of necessity that He create man in His image and likeness. Only by existing in the same dimension of glory could man legally serve as a companion of God. This is the same principle that is found in the New Testament, where the apostle John declares:

> God is light and in Him is no darkness at all. If we say that we have fellowship with Him, and walk in darkness, we lie and do not practice the truth. But if we walk in the light as He is in the light, we have fellowship with one another, and the blood of Jesus Christ His Son cleanses us from all sin.
>
> —1 JOHN 1:5–7

The most devastating consequence of sin is that it separates us from companionship with God. How empty life is for the image bearer who has been separated from The Image Maker. How lonely his world is when he no longer hears the voice of his Father whispering in the cool of the day. Man was originally created in the presence of glory and will only be fulfilled when he lives life in that same glory. The glory of God is to the spirit of man what natural air is to the lungs of man.

Man was created to be in covenant with other men. Verse 26 says, "Let Us make man," and verse 27 confirms the act by saying, "So God created man." In the first instance, the whole human race is in mind; in the latter, the first family—Adam and Eve—have been created. The nondescript picture of mankind gives way to the identifiable father and mother of the human race. Identifying the first individual in this manner opens the door for the introduction of woman. The woman did not evolve from or grow out of the man. She was created in the image of God, out of the substance of man.

This principle is clarified in Genesis 2, which describes the creation of Eve: "The LORD God said, 'It is not good that man should be alone; I will make him a helper comparable to him'" (v. 18). This description reveals how the woman is called to rule in conjunction with her husband. Her status is not that of a second-class citizen. She is not confined by cultural constraint or the insecurity of weak men. Eve was free to live as an image bearer.

A careful study of this passage in light of the New Testament reveals that God created the man and woman redemptively equal but functionally different. Their relationship was to serve as a pattern for every other relationship that would follow thereafter.

Anthony Hoekema describes their relationship in these words: "The man-woman relationship, therefore, implies the need for fellowship between human beings. But what is said in Genesis 1 and 2 about this relationship has implications also for our relationship to our fellowmen in general."[8] Man was formed as a relational creature with an inherent need to be needed. Kingdom relationships frame the meaning of life.

I believe that God's design for the family is a pattern for the basic relational structure of every institution that exists under the government of heaven. Every authority structure in the universe is to be formed out of the very components that make up the family structure. The social structures of society—the civil, commercial and even the religious structures of man—are to be established and governed according to the design God has provided. No other pattern will be successful in producing kingdom results. The Image Maker has given only one plan for relational interaction. No other substitute plan or modification will ever bring true peace into the human condition.

The enemy's schemes have so polluted contemporary society that God's plan seems foreign to most people. There is even the temptation for the most conservatively minded people to modify the plan of God in order to conform more closely to the society in which they live. But as different as God's plan may seem to some, it is the only pattern that will bring the results mankind desires. In the long run, every other alternative lifestyle will eventually lead to poverty of soul and to death, because any modification to God's original blueprint will not stand the test of time. Modification means destruction!

Man was created to be in covenant with creation. Standing beside her husband, Eve became a recipient of the very same mandate Adam was given. The Scripture reveals their earthly inheritance in the commission to establish dominion. Genesis 1:28 says, "God blessed them, and God said to them [*ish* and *isha*, male and female], '…have dominion….'" Adam and Eve were not created to rule alone, independent of each other; they were commissioned to exercise joint dominion. As a result of the dominion mandate, ruling became a shared responsibility.

Let me ask you a question. What is dominion? The

40

Amplified Version defines it as "authority." The New American Standard describes it as "rule." In light of my understanding of the message of the kingdom, I prefer the term "government." When the Scripture speaks of exercising dominion, it is referencing the establishment of the "government" of God.

It has been said that the greatest question of our day is, "Who's in charge here?" Mankind is wrestling over the issue of spiritual authority in the seventh millennium. We are currently engaged in a battle that will determine the spiritual and social agenda among the nations. Who will determine the course of history—will it be materialism, atheism, post-modernism or cosmic humanism, or will the kingdom of God be demonstrated?

When I speak of exercising dominion, I'm not referring to fleshly militant overthrow. The dominion mandate reveals the inseparable connection between ruling and stewarding. As we work our way into proceeding chapters, you will discover that the new creation is called to change the nations through the power of serving. It is becoming increasingly evident that God is giving us the opportunity to disciple entire nations in our lifetime. We are called to demonstrate the triumph of the last Adam (the Lord Jesus Christ) over the works of darkness in our generation.

The Image Maker did not create the world for demons. He did not invest His life, love and creative energy on behalf of angels. The Image Maker designed the world to be governed by mankind, and He will not finalize the historical scenario until redeemed man (under the lordship of Jesus Christ) exercises full dominion in the earth.

REVEALING THE GRAND DESIGN

As PAUL STOOD on Mars Hill surrounded by the symbols of humanism (the philosophers), atheism (the Epicureans) and pantheism (the Stoics), his spirit was provoked to anger at the irrational nature of these idol worshipers. One ancient writer identified thirty thousand different gods in Athens. Petronius, one of the ancient historians, said that it was easier to find a god in Athens than a man. In their attempt to suffice the anger of every cosmic deity, these pagans even built an altar with the inscription "TO THE UNKNOWN GOD." Ironically, it was the Athenians who considered Paul to be demonically inspired because of his message concerning the resurrection of Jesus Christ.

In Paul's discourse to these superstitious idolaters, he boldly confirmed their poetic concept of the identity of man. Drawing from the writings of a pantheistic poet, Paul said, "As also some of your own poets have said, 'For we are also His offspring.' Therefore, since we are the offspring of God, we ought not to think that the Divine Nature is like gold or silver or stone, something shaped by art and man's devising" (Acts 17:28–29).

What an incredible statement! Paul affirms the dignity of man by acknowledging that man is God's offspring, created in His image. As Ray Steadman once said, "It is not biblical to go around telling people that man is nothing, that he is vile, that he is a worm and so forth. This is not the biblical view of man as he was created."

Let there be no mistake about it, mankind is still the offspring of God. In spite of the rebellion of man and his tragic fall from grace, the image of God continues to exist upon the face of all mankind. But the image of God alone is not sufficient for our salvation. We must recover the beauty and power of a life lived in His likeness. We must begin the long journey home.

We have settled for a subnormal existence. In reality, we don't know how far man has fallen, but we do have the road map back to full restoration.

Three

THE LONG
JOURNEY HOME

We shall not cease from exploration
And the end of all our exploring
Will be to arrive where we started
And know the place for the first time.
—T. S. ELLIOT

I T ALL BEGAN in the Garden. Adam and Eve lived in the sinless state of untried perfection. Without fear or shame, they delighted themselves in creation, in each other and in the presence of The Image Maker. Each day was a new adventure filled with the discovery of unnamed animals and unexplored geography. Every new vista revealed unseen dimensions of God's forethought in the formation of creation. And then there was Eden.

Eden was the pattern environment for the whole of the earth. It served as the prototype of every other community that was to be constructed, structured and governed by Adam and Eve. This pristine garden served as a command post from which they were to launch their mission to conquer, rule and steward the whole of the earth. It was a taste of heaven in the midst of hostile surroundings. Even as the river of Eden flowed out of the Garden carrying life to the north, south, east and west, so were Adam and Eve destined to carry the glory of God to the four corners of the planet.

Then suddenly, without provocation or warning, it all changed, forever. Into the tranquil beauty of this innocent garden, sin came sneaking, carefully hidden in lying words and manipulated images. The serpent selectively recalled the words of The Image Maker, ignoring their context and distorting their meaning.

"You will be like God," the serpent told the woman, inciting desires and emotions that she had never experienced before. If this were true, she rationalized, then life could be even better than it presently was. Her curiosity gave birth to lust, and when lust was conceived, to disobedience. Adam willingly joined her in the ultimate act of betrayal against The Image Maker with his eyes wide open. His transgression was firmly rooted in the idolatry of loving and trusting the woman more than the Creator, who gave her to him. Although Adam and Eve were created in God's image and likeness, they were subject to the authority of God (Gen. 1:26). The promise of the serpent was that Adam and Eve would become coequal with God. The battle was over the issue of submission. Would they yield to the authority of God's sovereign will, or would they presume to know better than God?

The fall of Adam and Eve into sin was not just an isolated act of disobedience against God, but an act of high treason against the whole of creation. Just as creation rejoiced in their formation, creation also grieved in their transgression and subsequent alienation from the Garden. The effects of sin were not confined to the "private lives" of the first family. Their personal sin had universal implications. Their private actions affected the whole of society. Nothing was isolated from, and insulated against, the destructive force of unrighteousness working against the original design and purpose. Everything in the created order was affected by the corrosive work of sin in the earth. According to the Scriptures, "...the creation (nature) was subjected to frailty (to futility, condemned to frustration), not because of some intentional fault on its part..." (Rom. 8:20, AMP).

The obvious effects of the Fall are everywhere around us. Whether we examine the social structures of family, state and church, or the cultural aspects of art, science and technology, we find continual degeneration rather than regeneration. The river no longer flows from the Garden.

Multnomah professor David Needham describes the Fall of man in classic terms:

> Though some writers focus on what Adam and Eve gained—a sin nature—when they fell, the biblical emphasis is on what they lost. There, under the tree of the knowledge of good and evil, Adam and Eve not only lost the hope of immortality (the tree of life), but by choice they lost a dependency-linkage to God life. They became "alienated from the life of God" (Eph. 4:18).[1]

After the Fall of man, the image of God was not obliterated, but rather distorted. Although Adam continued to reflect a distorted image of the character of God, he no longer revealed the likeness of God. Perhaps the point could be clarified with a simple illustration. Several years ago, my wife and I were walking the streets of a major tourist attraction when we saw an artist drawing caricatures of the tourists. After much coaxing (and perhaps a little feminine manipulation), I finally agreed to have my picture drawn.

Fifteen minutes later I was holding a charcoal drawing of a caricature that grossly exaggerated my most prominent feature. Riding on a skateboard, with a giant head and a diminutive body, there I was, grinning foolishly in black and white. The size of my head was only eclipsed by the length of my nose, which, to scale, must have been at least three feet long!

This is a picture of the effect of sin on the image of God in the life of man. The presence of sin has distorted the original image of man. Although he still reveals certain recognizable features of the image of God, he is a caricature of his former self. This distortion has diminished his ability to mirror effectively The Image Maker. The eighteenth-century French philosopher Voltaire cynically declared, "God made man in His image, and man returned the favor."

A human being after the Fall, though marred by sin, is still a human being. His humanity was not reduced down to the level of a lesser primate. He is a fallen man—not a risen ape. While revealing certain aspects of his original image, fallen man has imposed his selfish desires upon his most prominent features. Where his original image once reflected the capacity to love unselfishly, fallen man now loves when it best serves his own desire. Where his original image once reflected the righteousness of The Image Maker, fallen man now seeks to establish his righteousness apart from God. Where his original image once revealed the meaning and purpose of life, fallen man now wrestles over the reason for his existence. Where his original image once revealed unconditional acceptance, man now struggles to find his ultimate worth.

Fallen man, at his best, is only capable of revealing brief glimpses of his former self. Like brief images flitting across a television screen between the grainy pictures of an interrupted signal, man occasionally reveals a faint picture of who he once was.

I think Herman Bavinck put it best when describing the present state of fallen man:

> Man through the fall…has not become a devil who, incapable of redemption, can no longer reveal the features of the image of God. But while he has remained really and substantially man and has preserved all his human faculties, capacities and powers, the form, nature, disposition and direction of all these powers have been so changed that now instead of doing the will of God they fulfill the law of the flesh.[2]

Under the influence of unrighteousness, new emotions replaced the love, peace and joy once found in the heart of man. He became vain in his imagination, and his foolish heart was darkened. Boasting of his personal wisdom, he became a fool, replacing the likeness of God with the actions of the evil one. (See Romans 1:20–23.) As man no longer related to one another based upon the grace of God, new feelings, never before experienced, became dominant in his emotions. For the first time in his life, he felt the strange sensations of fear, shame, insecurity and rejection. The entire human race enslaved within the seed of man began the downward spiral toward bondage and brokenness.

Although he was no longer subject to the personal counsel and guidance of The Image Maker, the image bearer continued to experience the longing for his original design and purpose. His inner longing was for companionship with his Creator. He desired meaningful interaction with other image bearers. His instinct to rule over creation was not abated.

Fallen man still longs for the fulfillment of the divine intention. Without the presence of The Image Maker, his life is left empty and void. Relationships are shallow and insignificant. Creation is worshiped rather than subdued.

REJECTED AND REMOVED

Then the LORD God said, "Behold, the man has become like one of Us, to know good and evil. And now, lest he put out his hand and take also of the tree of life, and eat, and live for ever"—therefore, the LORD God sent him out of the garden of Eden to till the ground from which he was taken. So He drove out the man; and He placed cherubim at the east of the garden of Eden, and a flaming sword which turned every way, to guard the way to the tree of life.

—GENESIS 3:22–24

Imagine the emotional pain of being rejected by the infinite Architect of the universe. Adam was not simply rejected by friends or family, he was rejected by the lover of his soul, the cultivator of his potential, the guardian of his destiny. The Image Maker rejected Adam without even giving him a second chance to redeem himself. There is no form of rejection any greater than the devastation of having been rejected by God Himself.

Because of our position in this situation and our perspective on the events that transpired, most of us identify with Adam's pain more than we do with God's. As a matter of fact, it is difficult for us to even understand God's capacity for pain. *How can God feel pain?* we wonder.

Yet the Scriptures reveal the emotional dimension of The Image Maker on more than one occasion. I cannot even comprehend the pain of separation that God must have experienced as Adam rejected Him. Imagine the pain God must have experienced as creation rebelled against Creator—as God was rejected, even disenfranchised from His very image and likeness.

Philip Yancey captured the emotional picture for us when he wrote:

> I sometimes wonder how hard it has been for God not to act in history. How must it feel to see the glories of creation—the rain forests, the whales, the elephants—obliterated one by one? How must it feel to see the Jews themselves nearly annihilated? To lose a son? What is the cost of God's self-restraint? I had always thought of the Fall in terms of its effects on us humans, namely the penalties outlined in Genesis 3. This time I was struck by its effect on God.[3]

On the surface, Adam's transgression may appear to be a case of rebellion rather than rejection. And yet what we cannot seem to grasp in this generation is that to rebel against the Word of God is, in fact, to reject God Himself. We live in a culture that attempts to piecemeal out the gospel, accepting the parts we like and rejecting the parts we don't, while still maintaining friendship with God. But the truth is: You cannot reject the Word of God and still be His buddy. If you reject the principles of life, then your friendship with God is only a figment of your imagination!

Adam not only rejected the law of life, but in doing so he rejected the Author of life. From God's perspective, this was not like being rejected by a distant relative you didn't really care for to begin with. This was not like being ostracized by a peer group that you had no interest in joining to begin with. Adam's rebellion was the highest level of rejection ever seen in the universe. This was far more devastating than the rebellion of Lucifer and the revolt of the angels.

The Image Maker was rejected by the very one formed in His image. The one who carried His genes, understood His heart and walked with Him in the cool of the day had abandoned Him. His closest confidant, who once shared in His dream for the future, had suddenly without warning or provocation deserted Him. The image bearer, who lived in His presence without shame, could no longer meet His eyes.

This was not a separation over irreconcilable differences. This was not a divorce in a loveless marriage—this was more akin to physical dismemberment. This was like losing a part of your essential identity. We've all heard the stories of amputees who, subsequent to surgery, experienced "phantom pains." The sensation of a cramping calf muscle after a leg has been removed; the sensation of tickling on the bottom of a foot that is no longer there; the instinct to clasp your hands even though one is missing—these are signs of "phantom pains."

I wonder what it was like for God to lose Adam? What did He think about in the cool of the day? What has He thought about every evening for six thousand years?

THE PRINCIPLE OF THE SEED

BEGINNING WITH THE sin of Adam in the Garden of Eden, rejection entered into the human condition and has continued to foster insecurity, isolation and intimidation in every generation since. This is the *principle of the seed* at work in the course of human history. The *principle of the seed* is simply this: *You were present even when you were not present.* According to this principle, you were present in the Garden, in Adam, before you were even born. That's why the apostle Paul declares, "For as by one man's disobedience many were made sinners, so also by one Man's obedience many will be made righteous" (Rom. 5:19).

The immediate question that springs to mind is this: How can I be held accountable for a crime committed before I was even born? I have often heard people complain, saying, "It just doesn't seem fair that I have to pay for Adam's sin!" This is the "seed factor" at work. I concede that it doesn't seem fair, but neither was it fair for Jesus to pay the penalty for our transgression with His life.

I believe we can best understand our identity in Christ by facing our identity in Adam. When we were born into this world, we were born into a kingdom, a family and a spiritual ethnicity. We had no choice in the matter. Perhaps it seems unfair that we should be judged for a sin that we didn't personally commit, in a place we've never been, with people we've never met. But no one ever promised that life would be fair. Life isn't fair, but God is just.

Even though the "seed factor" worked *against* us in Adam, it worked *for* us in Christ. We were chosen as His "spiritual seed"; we were in Him when He was crucified, buried and resurrected. Paul said, "For if by the one man's offense many died, much more the grace of God and the gift by the grace of the one Man, Jesus Christ, abounded to many" (Rom. 5:15).

PERFORMANCE-BASED REJECTION

LET'S CONTINUE THE long journey home. Genesis 4 contains one of the most tragic narratives in the whole of Scripture. Here we discover the record of the first murder in the history of mankind. But more importantly, this passage is the backdrop to every religious war that has existed since then. Cain murdered Abel over a difference of opinion concerning how God should be worshiped.

One generation removed from man's creation and complete acceptance by God, Cain was striving to gain God's favor. Fallen man digressed from *relationship-based* acceptance to *performance-based* acceptance. And in the process, this first family has deteriorated from being fully functional human *beings* to fully dysfunctional human *doings*.

Rather than being admitted into the presence of The Image Maker based upon divine design (their essential identity), Adam's family is now struggling to be admitted based upon performance.

The Fall not only affected Adam's relationship with The Image Maker, it also affected his personhood. No longer insulated from the serpentine effects of doubt, confusion and disillusionment, Adam and Eve began to struggle with shame and rejection.

C. S. Lewis describes the aftershock of the Fall in this manner:

> The process [of the Fall of Adam] was not, I conceive, comparable to mere deterioration as it may now occur in a human individual; it was a loss of status as a species. What condition was transmitted by heredity to all later generations, for it was not simply what biologists call an acquired variation. It was the emergence of a new kind of man; a new species, never made by God, *had sinned its way into existence*...It was a radical alteration of His constitution.[4]

Looking at your family photo album may convince you that you were born into the poster family for dysfunctionalism. Guess what? You are exactly right! But not because you were born into the Crist family or the Williams family or the Johnson family. Your dysfunctionalism stems from your birth into Adam's family. Your birth into fallen humanity is more fundamental to your identity than your immediate family.

One of the most popular television programs of the mid-1960s was an eerie show about a creepy family called *The Addams Family*. Replete with strange habits and disgusting relatives, they quickly worked their way into the heart of most television viewers. Why? Without overanalyzing this trivial moment in American television history, I would suggest that it was because most people could identify with the hyperbole. After all, we all have habits that are annoying and relatives we would like to keep hidden.

MOVING IN THE WRONG DIRECTION

> This is the book of the generations of Adam. In the day when God created man, He made him in the likeness of God. He created them male and female, and He blessed them and named them Man in the day when they were created. When Adam had lived one hundred and thirty years, he became the father of a son in his own likeness, according to his image, and named him Seth.
>
> —GENESIS 5:1–3, NAS

Although Adam was created in the image and likeness of God, his son Seth bore the image and likeness of Adam in his fallen state. I believe this passage gives further credence to the subtle differences between the words *image* and *likeness*. Seth was not only born with the physical characteristics of his father, he also carried his propensity to act in a certain manner. Adam's "fallenness" was spiritually and genetically transferred to the next generation. The likeness of God was perfect. The likeness of Adam was imperfect. The likeness of God was righteous. The likeness of Adam was unrighteous. Every living being upon the face of this planet now bears the likeness of fallen man.

As Emil Brunner once wrote:

> Man's relation with God, which determines his whole being, has not been destroyed by sin, but it has been perverted. Man does not cease to be the being who is responsible to God, but his responsibility has been altered from a state of being in love to a state of being under the law, a life under the wrath of God.[5]

55

FALLEN AND FRUSTRATED

LET'S CONTINUE ON our journey. After eradicating the sinful presence of fallen man through the floodwaters of judgment, God entered into a New Covenant with Noah. You may be interested to discover that every covenant God has entered into with man, since the Adamic covenant, is just an expanded version of that original covenant. God's covenant with Noah contained the same basic components of Adam's covenant. God's covenant with Abraham was basically an expanded version of the original covenant. God's covenant with Israel was basically the same covenant. The New Covenant with the church is essentially the same covenant. Through each new covenant, God is still searching for a man who will manage the planet on His behalf.

After the floodwaters abated, Noah planted a vineyard, harvested some grapes, fermented a bottle of wine and passed out naked in his tent where Ham (his youngest son) walked in on him. Noah awakened in a stupor and cursed the lineage of Ham for his transgression. In one moment of rage Noah rejected his son and cursed his descendants.

Can you see how the cycle of dysfunctionalism continues from one generation to the next? God chose a grace-filled man by the name of Noah and destroyed the original environment that contained the rejection of Adam and Eve. Yet this grace-filled man still struggled with the issues of acceptance and rejection because of the human condition into which he had been born!

Noah was several generations removed from Adam, and yet the sin continued on. In spite of the newly renovated earth, the force of rejection was still present, because sin is not a product of environment. Rejection is a product of the rebellion that produced the disenfranchisement of the whole human race. Rejection was built into the human condition.

Noah's reaction was not a product of environment, as some pop-psychologists would have you believe. You can be born into the most loving and nurturing environment and still struggle with these issues of acceptance and affirmation, because rejection has been built into your genetic makeup. This condition was no longer confined to Adam, Cain and the descendants of Ham. Rejection is now a human condition. Wherever you find humans, you will find men and women struggling with the issues of identity, affirmation, self-worth and acceptance.

A VITAL DISCOVERY

MISTAKEN IDENTITY ALWAYS results in a wrong behavior. As a matter of fact, mistaken identity always results in a behavior out of accord with one's true identity. For the sake of illustration, let me describe it this way. If you can convince a man that he is a slave—when in fact he is a king by birth—then he will develop a slave mentality and will live far beneath his inherited right. In spite of who he is genetically, in spite of his heritability, he will never rise to the throne because he believed a lie concerning his identity. Who you are determines how you act.

At the risk of sounding redundant, I want to rephrase that example. If you can convince a man that he is a pauper—when in fact he is the heir to a vast fortune—then that man will live in psychological and spiritual impoverishment because he believed a lie concerning his essential identity. In spite of his legal right to live in prosperity, he will settle for less than he is entitled to possess.

Long before the language of "self-esteem" ever worked its way into the pop-psychology culture, the Bible identified the principle of self-image as the key to fulfilling one's destiny. The wisest man who lived phrased it this way: "For as he [man] thinks in his heart, so is he" (Prov. 23:7).

THE DESTINATION IS IN SIGHT

WE HAVE SETTLED for a subnormal existence. In reality, we do not know just how far man has fallen, but we do have the road map back to full restoration. We are in the process of getting our memory back. We are in the process of rediscovering whom and what God originally designed us to be.

I believe God is going to have a generation that finalizes the struggle that was begun in the Garden of Eden. The generation of the last Adam will ultimately repair and rebuild everything forfeited and destroyed by the first Adam.

There is a world waiting to be born, a world in which righteousness prevails. A world in which believers live secure in their identity as sons and daughters of the kingdom. A world in which sickness and disease hide in fear before the believer who is confident in his sonship. A world in which men cooperate with the Holy Spirit in unprecedented dimensions. A world renovated by the fire of the Holy Spirit.

It all began in the Garden, and it is destined to end with some generation. Why not let it be ours?

Only as we "live and move and find our being" in Him will we discover whom we were really meant to be. Our identity is clearly linked to His existence in the world.

Four

BACK TO EDEN
AND BEYOND

I T IS IMPOSSIBLE to ignore the widespread effect of the Fall on our world. The results of Adam's transgression are as obvious as the signs of the times. The distinctiveness of both the male and female gender is under question as men and women struggle to accept the divine design for mankind. The creational institution of marriage is suffering under incredible attack as men and women selfishly demand personal "rights" at the expense of self-sacrifice and family responsibility. The family is severely strained by the disruptive forces of materialism and greed. Our global economy is fragile and susceptible to sudden collapse. Political systems, originally called to serve the purpose of God by making known His ways, have become corrupted through pride and rebellion. Culture of the twenty-first century is used as a weapon against the presence of God rather than as an instrument to glorify Him. And then there is the human condition.

There is a radical difference between the way you were originally created and the way you were finally born. The Image Maker originally designed you to live in righteousness, but you were "born in sin and shaped in iniquity." (See Psalm 51:5.) You were created to rule and reign, but you entered life as a slave to unrighteousness. You were constructed in the image of excellence but born into a world of dysfunction. Mankind was formed in progressive life but born into gradual death.

The apostle Paul describes our condition this way, "Therefore, just as through one man sin entered the world, and death through sin, and thus death spread to all men, because all sinned" (Rom. 5:12).

As I stated in the previous chapter, I don't think we realize just how far we've fallen. The sin of the man affected far more than his status with the Creator. In one moment of time, Adam forfeited everything of worth and value, leaving humanity naked and ashamed outside the Garden.

Our fallenness does not only work against the personal destiny to which we have been called, but it also works to abort the purpose of those things entrusted to our care. Our stewardship skills were directly affected by the Fall. Apart from the wisdom of God in our lives, we are bound to mismanage things of worth and value. Left to ourselves, we will govern the whole of life according to the ways of fallen man, rather than stewarding life according to the heavenly pattern.

After being separated from God, man's primary relationship with the spirit world shifted. Rather than relating to

The Image Maker as the Father of life, men sought to dwell in darkness in order to hide their wicked deeds. As a result, their understanding was corrupted and their foolish hearts were darkened. (See Romans 1:21; Ephesians 4:18.) No longer drawing their spiritual nourishment from the original source of supply, they began to draw strength from a counterfeit source. Mankind was now "dead in trespasses and sins" (Eph. 2:1).

To be spiritually dead is to be alienated from the life source of heaven. Yet, just like the 1968 "cult film," *Night of the Living Dead,* man did not recognize his own state of being. He became a spiritual zombie. Walking through life with the preprogrammed movements of a robot, he retained just enough of the image of God to enable him to fulfill a portion of the dominion mandate. Life was reduced to the desire to procreate and to self-preserve.

Instead of discovering the meaning for existence within the framework created by The Image Maker, man looked for purpose in illegitimate sources. The "gods of this world" obscured the ultimate meaning of life, as human life was defined by intellectualism, materialism and sensualism. (See 2 Corinthians 4:4.)

As man continued to drink of the contaminated waters of counterfeit life, he withdrew further from the presence of The Image Maker and strengthened his relationship with the usurper, Satan. This perverted association became man's defining agency, so when Jesus looked at Adam's spiritually dead descendants, He said, "You are of your father the devil, and the desires of your father you want to do" (John 8:44). Man's primary relationship had changed from The Image Maker to the image defiler.

Perhaps the clearest Scripture defining the relationship of fallen man to Satan is found in Ephesians 2:3. Paul describes mankind by saying, "We ... were by *nature* children of wrath" (emphasis added). This fallen nature was our very life. Man was born from the womb of disobedient woman, thereby forming him in a state of unrighteousness. Our life source was firmly rooted in the "prince of the power of the air," and our actions were those of "the children of disobedience." (See Ephesians 2:2.) We became the bastard human race. We existed without any meaningful relationship to the Father of creation.

Paul continues on to chronicle the history of fallen man, saying that we "lived" in unrighteousness. (See Ephesians 2:5.) Notice the fatal paradox that is described to us. Fallen man *lives*, "*dead* in trespasses and sins." How can one be both alive and dead at the very same time? This incongruity describes our condition—fallen man exists apart from the source of life. Man is disconnected from the true origin of life and reconnected to *pseudo*life. In our blindness to the original design, we settled for a counterfeit form of existence. Apart from faith in Christ, fallen man is the walking dead, alienated from the source of true life and estranged from his ultimate worth and value.

I've often imagined that when the "fullness of time was come," The Image Maker looked at the tragic condition of fallen man and said, "The earth is filled with a generation of men that I created but did not father." The only way to renew the fathering relationship was to restore the family connection. But in order to reinstate the image bearer to his original condition in the image *and* likeness of God, man needed to be reborn. The Son of God was sent from heaven to open up a spiritual birth canal through which we might be born from above.

DISCOVERING THE TRUE YOU

IN HIS PARAPHRASE of the New Testament titled *The Message*, Eugene Peterson translates John 1:11–13 to read, "He

[Jesus] came to his own people, but they didn't want him. But whoever did want him, who believed he was who he claimed and would do what he said, *he made to be their true selves*, their child-of-God selves. These are the God-begotten, not blood-begotten, not flesh-begotten, not sex-begotten" (emphasis added).

What a powerful thought! Through the miracle of spiritual regeneration, Jesus made us to be our *true* selves. Have you ever felt as though you were not reaching your full potential in life? Have you ever struggled to discover who you really are? Is there a part of you so deeply buried that you have never felt free to express it to your closest friends? The answer to discovering your true identity is found in Jesus Christ. Only as we "live and move and find our being in Him" will we discover whom we were really meant to be. Our identity is clearly linked to His existence in the world.

The implication found in John 1:12 is that we existed in a substandard state, far beneath the divine design for our lives. Only through the new birth experience can we be brought back to our new selves, our *true* selves.

I am convinced that fallen man is suffering from memory loss. Sin has obliterated our memory, leaving us without a clear sense of our ultimate worth. We have forgotten who we are and why we are alive. The memory of our former selves (mankind before the Fall) can only be regained through the process of spiritual regeneration.

A. W. Tozer once said:

> The truth received in power shifts the basis of life from Adam to Christ, and a new set of motives goes to work within the soul. A new and different Spirit enters the personality and makes the believing man new in every department of his being.[1]

CREATED ONCE, BORN TWICE

ALONE AND IN the dark, a man silently slipped through the streets of Jerusalem. As the flickering candlelight nimbly worked its way through the thin curtains carefully hung in the small homes lining the passageway, it cast his shadow on the wall of the narrow corridors defining the streets of the old city. Shivering with fear and damp with perspiration, he pondered the possible consequences of the mission upon which he had embarked. As a Jewish rabbi, a long-standing member of the Sanhedrin and one of the wealthiest men in the community, the repercussions could be devastating. Nevertheless he swallowed his fear, lengthened his stride and continued to search for the Teacher.

Nicodemus had everything to lose, but even more to gain. Risking his reputation, he sought for the answer common to all men. Who really was this man called Jesus of Nazareth? Was He the long-awaited Messiah or something less than God's only begotten Son? The answer Jesus gave perplexed him even more. "Except a man be born again, he cannot see the kingdom of God" (John 3:3, KJV).

Seeing the confused look on the face of Nicodemus and hearing the question "How can a man be born when he is old?", Jesus continued on. "Flesh gives birth to flesh, but the Spirit gives birth to spirit" (v. 7, NIV). Suddenly, in a burst of revelation, the answer became clear. What Jesus was proposing was far greater than the vague, symbolic ritual that was commonly required of those converting to Judaism or even some pagan religion. Jesus was speaking of an actual, revolutionary change in a man's essential being.

When Jesus spoke of being "born again," he used the Greek phrase *gennao anothen*, which can be translated literally as "born from above." This is much more substantial than joining a church or even making a conscious decision to live a different kind of lifestyle. This transformation is so radical that it can only be defined in those terms, which describe the principles of procreation and birth! This is the supernatural process that brings us back to Eden and beyond. The quality of life we now find in Christ is spiritually superior to the life that Adam lived.

- You were born the first time by the will of man, but the second time by the will of God.

- The first birth formed you in the image of God, but the second birth formed you in His likeness.

- The first birth created you by the blood of man; the second birth created you by the blood of Jesus Christ.

A RADICAL PERSPECTIVE

I RECENTLY DISCOVERED a remarkable book by Philip Yancey and Dr. Paul Brand titled *Fearfully and Wonderfully Made*. When speaking of the new birth, the authors declare:

> I can only fathom the concept of being visited by the living Christ by considering its parallel in the physical world: the mystery of life in which DNA passes on an infallible identity to each new cell. Christ has infused us with spiritual life that is just as real as natural life… The difference between a person joined to Christ and one not joined to Him is as striking as the difference between dead tissue and my organic body. DNA has organized chemicals and minerals to form a living, growing body, all of whose parts possess its unique corporate identity. In a parallel way, God uses the materials and genes of natural man, splitting them apart and recombining them with his own spiritual life.[2]

Notice carefully the use of the phrase "in a parallel way." I doubt if these authors believe the new birth experience affects the natural physiological makeup of man any more than I do. Unfortunately, because of the limitation of our human vocabularies we must use imperfect terms to describe spiritually perfect processes. Although the science of genetics was not defined or labeled as a "science" until the early 1940s, these principles have existed in the heart of the Father since the beginning of time. The Image Maker's intention has always been to have a family in His image and after His likeness who express His character and conduct to the world.

Philip Yancey continues on to say:

> The Designer of DNA went on to challenge the human race to a new and higher purpose—membership in His own body. And that membership begins with stuff-exchange, analogous to an infusion of DNA, for each cell in the body. The community called Christ's body differs from every other human group. Unlike a social or political body, membership in it entails something as radical as a new coded imprint inside each cell…This unfathomable idea of an actual identity exchange is implicit in conversion. Jesus described the process in terms His hearers could understand. To Nicodemus, He called it being "born again" or "born from above," indicating that *spiritual life requires an identity change as drastic as a person's first entrance into the world.*[3]

In order to enter the kingdom, man must become a different "spiritual species." No, the physical genetic encoding of man does not change. He is still born of woman and will continue to carry the fleshly genes of fallen man until the moment of final redemption, at which time this corruptible flesh will be transformed into an incorruptible body. As long as we are in the "flesh," we will continue to embody the physical characteristics of fallen man, which is flesh. However, the radical nature of spiritual regeneration actually transforms the hidden man of the inner heart, the spirit man, the eternal man, to such a degree that he becomes a brand-new man in Christ Jesus. That which is born of the Spirit is spirit.

As I stated in chapter two, God is a father, and a father cannot be defined apart from his children. The primary dream of the Father was to have a family in whose response His love could be expressed. So through the experience of the new birth, God takes humanity into partnership with Himself, allowing mere men to participate in the life that flows from heaven.

In his Classic Critical Concern book, *Birthright*, Professor David Needham describes the spiritual parallel found between physical conception and birth and the new birth process.

> By physical conception my parents gave me a "flesh" birth. It involved much more than my *getting* something. I *became* someone. I became a real, full-fledged, *flesh* person. Similarly, by the new birth, *I became a brand-new kind of person.* Jesus did not say being born again equals *getting* the Holy Spirit. He said it equaled *becoming* spirit.[4]

The point Needham seems to be making is that spiritual regeneration is not some type of religious appendage that God attaches to your old nature. It is the transformation of the old man into The Image Maker's new creation. Spiritual regeneration is the radical reconstruction of a person's essential identity. Jesus Christ actually forms a new spiritual man deep within the lives of those who receive Him as Lord.

THE LAW OF REPRODUCTION

IN ORDER TO fully comprehend what Jesus was saying to Nicodemus, you must understand the principle of reproduction in the construction of creation and the original formation of man. Everything in the created order was designed to reproduce after its own kind, according to Genesis 1. This "law of reproduction" even extended to the creation of man, when The Image Maker said, "Let Us make man in Our image, according to Our likeness" (Gen. 1:26).

Let me illustrate this principle for you by using a current event that my father-in-law shared with me from a recent magazine article. It seems that a group of scientists are presently teaching a gorilla to communicate by using American Sign Language.[5] The goal of the scientific study is to produce a gorilla that is capable of communicating independent thoughts and feelings. Now as fascinating as that may seem, the hard, cold truth is that when this experiment is completed, the scientific community will still have only a gorilla. He may be an intelligent gorilla. He may be a conversant gorilla. He may even get a job in public politics. But he is still nothing more than a gorilla. That which is flesh is flesh, that which is spirit is spirit— and that which is gorilla is gorilla!

Everything in the created order reproduces after its own kind. You cannot breed a male dog with a female hog and produce little doglets. Likewise, flesh cannot produce spirit, and spirit cannot produce flesh. Every species in the created order reproduces after its own kind. Even as man was originally created in the image and likeness of God, the new birth re-creates the spirit of man back into the image and likeness of God.

When a man gives up his arguments with God and surrenders his life to Jesus Christ, he instantly passes from "death unto life." One Christian writer put it like this: "Jesus is referring to the miracle that takes place when the divine activity remakes a man."[6]

In His role as the last Adam, Jesus came to restore the *likeness* of God back to the image bearer. This restoration could only be the result of a radical transformation at the core of fallen man. This transformation needed to be far greater than a change of perspective or even a new value system. Jesus Christ did not come to initiate anything less than full and complete conversion resulting in the regeneration of man. That's why J. Knox Chamblin could write with such boldness, "Jesus Christ is no less than the inaugurator of a new humanity."[7]

Listen to the way Paul describes the miracle of the new birth.

> Therefore, if anyone is in Christ, he is a new creation; old things have passed away; behold, all things have become new.
>
> —2 CORINTHIANS 5:17

You are, as the new creation, who you are whether you understand it or not, believe it or not or even act like it or not! When you surrendered your life to Jesus Christ, you were instantaneously reborn, regenerated, re-created, renewed and spiritually recoded. I am reasonably certain you walked away from that divine encounter reflecting the same physical image, but you were not the same. The hidden man of your inner heart had just been translated out of the kingdom of darkness, and during the course of that supernatural transition you became a brand-new person.

At the risk of belaboring the point, Arthur Custance describes this radical transformation in the following words:

> These two segments of the human race are at opposite

poles, they are basically in antithesis. They dwell together because they are both members of the *family* of man. They are one *genus*, to use the zoological term. But something has happened to cause them to separate into two *species* within that *genus*, and this separation is at a far deeper and more fundamental level than mere genetics. The division is the result of a spiritual transformation that really constitutes a new creation—nothing less, in fact, than rebirth.[8]

UNSOLVED MYSTERIES

IN INTERSPERSING SCIENTIFIC terms with biblical ones, I have probably opened Pandora's box and provoked more questions than I have answered. How can one be fully man, alive and in the flesh, and yet be fully re-created deep within the spirit realm? How can Christ dwell so completely in a man that the man no longer lives, but Christ? How can a man be both dead and alive at the very same time? Since the Word of God is the only qualified agent to fully distinguish and divide between soul and spirit, we are left to skirt around the edges in an attempt to discern between the two.

After wrestling with these issues for years, Paul the Apostle finally conceded that they are mysteries into which we are given glimpses.

> [Even] the mystery which has been hidden from ages and from generations, but now has been revealed to His saints. To them God willed to make known what are the riches of the glory of this mystery among the Gentiles: which is Christ in you, the hope of glory.
>
> —COLOSSIANS 1:26–27

These things seem difficult to grasp with human logic and natural reasoning because we are so accustomed to dealing with man at the lowest common denominator. We have seen man at his worst, alienated from God and without hope in this world. We have all witnessed the noble, but failed, attempt of religion to force Christlike conformity through rules and regulations. But have we ever seen a generation living out the reality of their essential identity in Christ Jesus? Have we seen a generation since the first-century church living in the power of new creation realities?

THE REDUCTION OF CHRISTIANITY

THE REASON I have chosen to emphasize this point so strongly is because far too many Christians have reduced the new birth experience down to the level of a self-improvement program. As a result, we find ourselves struggling with the very same issues that plague unbelieving society. We have fallen for the self-esteem trap rather than standing confident in our self-worth.

I firmly believe the greatest danger we face in the North American church is not over the *seduction* of Christianity but in the *reduction* of Christianity. In other words, I sincerely doubt if many genuine, Bible-believing Christians are in danger of renouncing their belief in the virgin birth of Christ or His physical, literal, bodily return. But scores of believers are confused as to the radical nature of the new birth experience. We have settled for a watered-down version of authentic New Testament Christianity. Even though Paul described us as "the new creation," deep down inside most of us still believe we are the same "old creation" with a new "Christian" title.

On a rare occasion, we actually meet someone bold enough to stand up and declare, "I have a new nature." That's a great start, but even that radical position pales in comparison to what the Scriptures have to say, because what you *have* isn't the point. It's not what you *have* that makes the ultimate difference, but *who* you are. We have been convinced that we're the same old person with a new set of friends and somewhere to go on Sunday morning! But we're not, and discovering the wonder of who we truly are will put an end to powerless living once and for all.

I am shocked at the number of born-again believers who cower before the princes of the world because they lack an understanding of their essential identity in Christ. It's no wonder that the image defiler continues his Garden exploits in an effort to keep the church blinded to our true identity. When we come to faith in who we really are, nothing shall withstand us. There is no force of darkness capable of withstanding the New Covenant man who understands who he truly is in God.

Although I made this point in an earlier chapter, the fact bears repeating. Mistaken identity always results in behavior out of accord with one's true identity. When we are uncertain about our identity, our mission is obscured. The dominion mandate is not being exercised by many who fill our church buildings today because they have settled for a distorted image of their ultimate worth and value. Even as unregenerate society struggles with the purpose of man in general, the church struggles to comprehend who we truly are as sons and daughters of the Most High God.

When men and women are born again, they are not accepted back into the presence of God as sinful humans who are permitted to visit on a trial basis. This, in essence, is the theological position of those holding the new creation in bondage to the sinful tendencies of their past. To them, Christianity has been reduced to the philosophy of Alcoholics Anonymous, which is "once an alcoholic, always an alcoholic." No, I am certainly not against Alcoholics Anonymous. This organization has helped many out of the bondage of alcoholism, and quite a number of those have even found God through their honest desire to deal with their addiction. But Jesus promised a new creation and a new identity to men when *born again,* not *reformed.*

As a matter of fact, the new birth experience is not about being "reformed"; it is about being spiritually "re-formed." This re-creation takes place in the spirit of man. Rather than accepting the lie of "once a sinner, always a sinner," we must come to believe that we truly "passed from death unto life" and that "all things have been made new." The church was not designed to serve as a support group for those who are attempting to gradually become Christian one day at a time. Spiritual regeneration is not a progressive experience. The new birth is not offered on the installment program. It is an instantaneous miracle.

I have counseled with countless Christians who are still struggling with some previous circumstance in their history. Some people struggle for decades over a demeaning violation of their sexuality while others contend with a breach of spiritual integrity. For many others, the battle is over abandonment and disappointment. Unfortunately, we are consigned to struggle with previous offenses until we discover that our past only has the influence that we allow it to have over our future.

Your deliverance is not going to be found in decades of psychotherapy or antidepressants. There is no lasting change in self-help seminars or motivational pep talks. The gospel alone contains the power of God unto salvation, deliverance, healing and restoration. Through trusting in the death, burial and resurrection of Jesus Christ, we are made brand-new.

After experiencing the radical nature of spiritual regeneration, you are transformed into a new person. There is not one single molecule of your former identity left after you have "passed from death unto life." You can use psychology to dig in the ashes of your former self, but remember that your former self was "crucified with Christ" and does not exist any longer. You can use distorted theology in an attempt to resurrect your former self, but heaven will not cooperate with your deformed perception. The good news is that you have been permanently altered at the core of your being.

The sum total of the Christian life was purchased for you on the cross of Calvary. Spiritually you have been given everything you need for the journey toward the "measure of the stature of the fullness of Christ." Tragically, many Christians are still waiting to *see* what redemption has already *revealed*. They are still waiting to possess what the cross legally gave us.

When I boldly speak of our position and our inheritance in Christ, I can see the horror reflected in the faces of those who do not understand this incredible opportunity. Let me explain it like this. Have you ever found yourself seated at the table in an expensive restaurant, only to look at the menu and discover that you really can't afford to eat there? Imagine receiving the menu in a fine French restaurant, only to realize that you can't afford to breathe the air, let alone eat a six-course meal. Suddenly, in a moment of panic, you slip out of your seat and bolt for the door, embarrassed and ashamed. Once out on the street, you vow never to allow yourself to be put in that position again. That is the same look I have seen on the faces of countless thousands who have been led to believe that they are responsible to pick up the bill and pay the tab on their own personal redemption!

AN IDENTITY CHANGE

AFTER WEIGHING THE evidence and considering the verdict, Paul the Apostle said:

> I am crucified with Christ: nevertheless I live; yet not
> I, but Christ liveth in me: and the life which I now live
> in the flesh I live by the faith of the Son of God, who
> loved me, and gave himself for me.
> —GALATIANS 2:20, KJV

Many Christians struggle with Paul's intended meaning because they have not considered the biblical principle of substitution. As He suffered and died on Mount Calvary, Jesus Christ became what He was not so that we might become what we were not. As He was crucified for our sins, Jesus Christ was made sin so that we might be made righteous. This is the divine exchange between God and man. This exchange does not simply leave us in a different spiritual state—it transforms us into a brand-new identity.

Everything that Jesus did He did so that you might be brought into the family of God. His mission was to redeem fallen man, offering them the opportunity to become the sons of the Most High God. The writer of Hebrews goes so far as to say:

> For it was an act worthy [of God] and fitting [to the
> divine nature] that He, for Whose sake and by Whom
> all things have their existence, *in bringing many sons
> into glory*, should make the Pioneer of their salvation
> perfect [should bring to maturity the human experi-
> ence necessary to be perfectly equipped for His office
> as High Priest] through suffering.
> —HEBREWS 2:10, AMP, EMPHASIS ADDED

HOW TO BECOME COMPLETE

THERE IS ONLY one person in the universe who is capable of completing you. You will never find completeness in your husband, wife or any other earthly relationship. The Fall of

Adam left you with an inherent desire to be "completed" by God alone. One Christian songwriter called this a "God-sized hole in every one of us." Many of us wandered through life trying everything in a futile attempt to "fill up" this inner vacuum. My generation's experimentation with drugs, alcohol and sexual promiscuity has been nothing more than self-medication. This is man's attempt to prescribe a remedy to fill his inner longing apart from faith in Jesus Christ.

There was an attempt in the first-century church, as in our present religious culture, to discover "completeness" apart from Christ. False teachers infiltrated this first-century church, encouraging a pilgrimage to wholeness through humanistic philosophy, with just enough of Jesus thrown in to make it sound legitimate. Paul counteracted this deception with instructions to avoid vain philosophy and empty deception.

> Beware lest any man spoil you through philosophy and vain deceit, after the tradition of men, after the rudiments of the world, and not after Christ. For in him dwelleth all the fulness of the Godhead bodily. And ye are complete in him, which is the head of all principality and power.
>
> —COLOSSIANS 2:8–10, KJV

Through the incredible gift of God's own Son, we are spiritually transformed and eternally complete. Jesus Christ is the only one capable of filling the deepest longing of your heart. He is the only one capable of repairing and rebuilding your broken self-image. The answer is not in a motivational seminar. The answer is not in human wisdom. The answer is not in religion. The answer is found in relationship with The Image Maker.

If you want to understand whom God originally created you to be, go back and research the life of Adam before the Fall. After you have developed a picture of Adam in his state of innocent righteousness, continue your study with the life of Jesus Christ. As the pattern Son, Jesus reveals the standard for our personhood and also for living life. We need to make the journey back to Eden and beyond. This process is only possible through the life, death and resurrection of the last Adam, who came to make things right.

PART II:
DISCOVERING YOUR
IDENTITY

The new creation is not simply clothed in the righteousness of Christ—the very ingredient that now makes up his essential identity is God's own righteousness.

Five

AWAKEN TO

RIGHTEOUSNESS

O NE OF THE most powerful moments in the New Testament was played out in a baptismal service in Bethabara. Waist deep in water, John carefully lowered his cousin into the Jordan River, thus fulfilling the scriptural mandate for Jesus to fulfill all righteousness. (See Matthew 3:15.) As a man born under the Old Covenant, the personal righteousness of Jesus Christ was directly linked to His ability to keep the Law of Moses.

Something very powerful and prophetic was at work in the baptism of Jesus. Not only do we have the greatest prophet who ever lived baptizing God's only begotten Son, but we also have the representative heads of both Covenants standing waist deep together in the Jordan River. Throughout Israel's history, this river prophetically stood as the symbol of adversity. When crossing the Jordan, Israel symbolically passed from failure to victory, from bondage to liberty, even from death to life. When exiting Egypt (a type of sin) and entering Caanan (the land of promise), the Israelites had to cross over the Jordan River. This one river symbolized their ongoing struggle to cross over every obstacle in their quest to fulfill their destiny.

Standing together in adversity, we discover the delegates of the Old and New Covenants, standing together in the greatest moment of transition that ever existed in the history of man. The birth order of the kingdom was changing. The New Covenant was being inaugurated, opening the door for a new expression of righteousness in the earth.

Shortly after this astounding event, Jesus said:

> Truly, I say unto you, among those born of women there has not arisen anyone greater than John the Baptist: yet he who is least in the kingdom of heaven is greater than he... For all the prophets and the Law prophesied until John.
>
> —MATTHEW 11:11, 13, NAS

In order to fully understand what Jesus was saying, we must ask ourselves a very important question. Why would Jesus distinguish John as *being born of woman?* Wasn't Jesus Himself born of woman? As a matter of fact, aren't all men born of women? Of course, the answer is yes; all men are born of women, but some men have gone on to the second birth, which is to be born of spirit. Remember what Jesus said to Nicodemus? "That which is born of the flesh is flesh, and that which is born of the Spirit is spirit" (John 3:6). John the Baptist was the greatest man who ever lived the life of the flesh.

It may be hard for you to reconcile this principle, but in the sight of God, all flesh is created equal, even though all flesh doesn't behave the same. Some people do a better job of governing their flesh than others do. I have been privileged to know some wonderful unsaved people who live moral, responsible, productive lives. They love their wives, father their children, pay their taxes and support humanitarian causes. But they are still living the life of the flesh. You may be living with disciplined flesh, but it's still flesh. You may be living with moral flesh, but it's still flesh.

Most Christians have this peculiar way of sorting and categorizing different sins, based upon their personal propensity toward them. We consider the sin of child abuse to be far more heinous than the sin of gossip. We believe that murder outranks bitterness. As a child, I grew up hearing my father repeat the phrase, "Sin is sin no matter who it's in." And it's true; that which is born of flesh is flesh. All flesh is created equal even though all flesh doesn't behave the same.

Jesus is showing us that up until this moment in history, the greatest man who ever lived the life of the flesh was John the Baptist. Evidently, John the Baptist was a master at managing his flesh life. He kept the Law of Moses and devoted his entire life to serving the purpose of God in his generation. Yet Jesus said, "He that is the least in the kingdom is far greater than John!" In other words, the *least* significant of the New Covenant species is far greater than the *most* significant of the Old Covenant species.

Jesus gave His life to birth the new creation of the Spirit, which is far greater than the old creation of the flesh. The central message of the New Testament is how the lost character of God in man has been restored through the substitutionary death, burial and resurrection of Jesus Christ. "The whole work of Jesus Christ in reconciliation and redemption may be summed up in the central conception of the renewal and consummation of the divine image in man."[1] The doctrine of reconciliation reveals the heart of the Father concerning the restoration of the image of man.

WHAT IS RIGHTEOUSNESS?

NEW COVENANT RIGHTEOUSNESS is far more than appropriate Christian conduct. Under the Law of Moses, righteousness was simply a matter of appropriate conduct. The Law seemed to be far more concerned with the behavior of man than with the condition of his heart. As long as one obeyed the rules, his heart could be resentful, bitter, lustful and unforgiving. This is the picture of the little boy who was corrected by his mother and sent to sit in the corner as a punishment for his disobedience. With his chin stubbornly set, his eyes glaringly defiant, he physically obeyed the law of his mother. But while passing through the room a few moments later, his mother heard him mutter, "I may be sitting down on the outside, but I'm standing up on the inside." The Law of Moses compelled fallen man to "sit down on the outside," but it did nothing to recondition the hidden man of the inner heart.

The Hebrew word for righteousness is the word *tsadaq*, which cannot be fully expressed with one English word. It literally means "stiff" or "straight," but it was also used to describe a "full measure or weight."[2] The Greek word for righteousness, *dikaiosune*, means "equity of character."[3] Both definitions of righteousness pertain to a standard of spiritual weights and measures.

Let me explain it like this. In 1901, the National Bureau of Standards (now known as the National Institute of Standards and Technology) was established by Congress to determine the criteria for all weights and measures in the United States of America. Before this national standard, one shopkeeper could determine a pound to be twelve ounces, and another could determine it to be fifteen ounces. One carpenter could define a foot as being seven inches long, and another craftsman could define it as being sixteen inches long. There was no scale by which the weights or measures could be judged. With the establishment of the national weights and measures law, it is now a federal offense to define an ounce, a pound, a gallon or an inch by any other measurement than that which has been legally determined.

In a spiritual sense, the Law of Moses contained the weights-and-measures standard for almighty God. It defined, on God's terms, what a full measure of righteousness was. No longer was man's responsibility toward God subject to personal opinion or individual interpretation. The Law defined the standard of conduct by which the whole earth was to be judged.

In the Old Testament, the matter of righteousness was always related to Jehovah, His Word, His character and His actions. And men were only referred to as "righteous" when their lives took on the same characteristics as were evidenced in God. Lest you think that God was setting man up for failure by requiring more than he was capable of performing, let me remind you that there actually were portions of the Law that were doable! Certain aspects of the Law were within the realm of possibility. (See Deuteronomy 27; 28; 30:9–11.)

PERFORMANCE-BASED RIGHTEOUSNESS

OLD COVENANT RIGHTEOUSNESS was performance-based righteousness. Like the modern-day concept of self-esteem, man's righteousness (worth and value) fluctuated from day to day based upon his accomplishment. The real tragedy with performance-based righteousness is that even if you succeed in keeping 99 percent of the Law, you still fail. You are condemned before the holiness of God, because "for whoever shall keep the whole law, and yet stumble in one point, he is guilty of all" (James 2:10).

Now this is where the real problem develops, because none of us are brazen enough to think that we can stand before the throne of almighty God based upon our good behavior and call that a full measure of righteousness. Ironically, our good behavior may, in fact, result in a form of righteousness (perhaps I should call it a *degree* of righteousness), but it isn't a full measure. It does not meet God's weights-and-measures standard, because the holiness of God demands a full measure of righteousness. This is how Paul distinguished between the incomplete measure of man's righteousness apart from the righteousness of God.

> For they being ignorant of God's righteousness, and seeking to establish their own righteousness, have not submitted to the righteousness of God.
>
> —ROMANS 10:3

This was the type of righteousness that Paul lived before his conversion on the road to Damascus. That's why he could say, "As for righteousness, my life has been faultless." (See Philippians 3:6.) And yet, it was to the very people who espoused this kind of righteousness that Jesus said, "You must be born again." Why? Because New Covenant righteousness is a different proposition altogether. New Covenant righteousness is the full measure of righteousness that comes of faith.

The righteousness that is of the law engages man in a life-and-death struggle for freedom—and yet it leaves him equipped for this battle with only the weapon of his will. The Law can only be kept by sheer force and determination. It produces absolutely no overcoming power, leaving man in a life-and-death struggle to remain above temptation and failure—a struggle with partial victories and countless defeats. It consists of great efforts to do good, to avoid evil and to please God by rising up from our failures and trying just to get it right the next time.

Yet in the end, legal, man-made righteousness is a terrible struggle mixed together with dreadful torment. Whenever temptation results in failure, we fall into total despair, as though God has finally forsaken us. And we become caught in an endless cycle of sin and confess, sin and confess...We are always uneasy in the presence of God, more aware of what we've done wrong than we are aware of what we've done right. We feel as though we never measure up.

Paul said in Romans 8:3–4:

> For what the law could not do in that it was weak through the flesh, God did by sending His own Son in the likeness of sinful flesh, on account of sin: He condemned sin in the flesh, that the righteous requirement of the law might be fulfilled in us who do not walk according to the flesh but according to the Spirit.

When we struggle to clothe ourselves in the righteousness of our own good works, we are consigned to stand before the holiness of God in filthy rags rather than in the beauty in which He has clothed us. Isaiah 64:6 declares that "all our righteousnesses [the righteousness that comes about by the law] are like filthy rags."

THE ONLY RIGHTEOUS MAN

As MAN FELL short of the divine standard generation after generation, the human race became deeper and deeper entrenched in iniquity and sin. Finally, because fallen man could not accomplish the standard required by the Law, The Image Maker sent His only begotten Image Bearer into the earth to fulfill the divine requirement.

The Father did everything He could to ensure mankind's reintegration into His spiritual family through sending His Son, Jesus, to die as the sacrifice needed to reconnect The Image Maker with His wayward children on the earth. Because of His mission of restoring and modeling the redeemed life, Jesus didn't live His life on earth as the royal descendant of the Creator of the universe, "the Son of God." Instead, the last Adam chose to live and demonstrate God's restoration plan as the "Son of Man." Jesus slept, became weary, hungered and felt pain in His incarnated humanity.

Jesus fulfilled the Law as a human being, not as a divine being. Although He was fully God, He laid aside His deity and lived in the reality of His humanity in order to satisfy the divine requirement for mankind. If Jesus had fulfilled the Law through the strength of His divinity, then justice would not have been served, and fallen man could not legally benefit from what He had accomplished. So He kept the Law as the "Son of Man" and fulfilled the righteous demands of almighty God. That's why He declared in Matthew 5:17, "Do not think that I came to destroy the Law or the Prophets. I did not come to destroy but to fulfill."

Jesus fulfilled the Law out of the motive of pure love in order to offer us the full measure of righteousness, which He secured through His obedience. It is impossible for God to accept any other righteousness than that which Jesus Christ offered to Him. No other man ever met the full requirements. Under the New Covenant there is now only one standard of weights and measures for perfect righteousness—the life of the Lord Jesus Christ.

NEW COVENANT RIGHTEOUSNESS

WHEREAS THE LAW offered performance-based righteousness, New Covenant righteousness is a different proposition altogether. New Covenant righteousness is the righteousness that comes through *faith*. This righteousness does not come to man through his good works, but through submission to the will of God. It is not a result of what you perform, but of whom you become. Johannas Behm in his *Theological Dictionary of the New Testament* says, "The new aeon (age) which has dawned with Christ brings a new creation, the creation of a new man."[4]

This new creation was made righteous as a result of trusting in the personal righteousness of Jesus Christ. Paul testified to the Philippians that He had exchanged the righteousness of the flesh for the righteousness that was of the Spirit.

> Yea doubtless, and I count all things but loss for the excellency of the knowledge of Christ Jesus my Lord: for whom I have suffered the loss of all things, and do count them but dung, that I may win Christ, and be found in him, not having mine own righteousness, which is of the law, but that which is through the faith of Christ, the righteousness which is of God by faith.
> —PHILIPPIANS 3:8–9, KJV

Did you see that? The key to New Covenant righteousness is contained in this one simple principle: When a man is found in Christ, he is judged righteous before God the Father. True righteousness is only found in one place in the universe, and that is in Christ. Outside of sharing in the life of Jesus Christ, you are relegated to living life according to your own personal righteousness—and that is a failing proposition. The Father cannot and will not accept your own personal righteousness, but He cannot and will not reject you when you are found in the righteousness of His Son.

When commenting on the issue of righteousness, David Needham writes:

> At the risk of oversimplification the difference between Old Covenant righteousness and New Covenant righteousness can be compared to the difference between "God as my helper" and "God as my life."[5]

The Old Covenant offers you a cosmic helper. The New Covenant offers you divine life.

BECOMING A RIGHTEOUS MAN

THIS NEW COVENANT righteousness is the evidence of the transformation that has taken place in the hidden man of the heart, in the life of the new creation. Your righteousness flows out of your identity as the new creation.

> Therefore if any man be in Christ, he is a new creature: old things are passed away; behold, all things are become new.... For he hath *made* him to be sin for us, who knew no sin; that we might be *made* the righteousness of God in him.
> —2 CORINTHIANS 5:17, 21, KJV, EMPHASIS ADDED

Paul the Apostle declares that the new creation is formed out of the righteousness of God's own character. He is not simply clothed in the righteousness of Christ, but the very ingredient that now makes up his essential identity is God's own righteousness. You see, not only do we have His righteousness covering our account, but we also have the very nature of righteousness spiritually fused into the new life of the new creation.

Philip Yancey has made this observation:

> This unfathomable idea of identity exchange is implicit in conversion...As a result of this stuff exchange, we carry within us not just the image of, or the philosophy of, or faith in, but the actual substance of God. One staggering consequence credits us with the spiritual genes of Christ: as we stand before God, we are judged on the basis of Christ's perfection, not our unworthiness.[6]

The very life and nature of God is righteousness, therefore the man who has received the nature of God now becomes the righteousness of God in Christ! I realize the armchair theologians may choke on this one, but I firmly believe that this righteousness becomes ours through spiritual imputation and infusion. Through "imputation" it satisfies the forensic need by appeasing the justice of almighty God. But it is also established in our lives by spiritual "infusion," thereby becoming a part of the spirit of the new creation.

Now think about this awesome concept for a moment as we further examine this principle. *To the degree that He was made sin, you were made righteous!* He became *what He was not,* in order that you might become *what you were not.* Jesus never committed sin. He was *made* sin. He did not become sin because He practiced sin. He became sin because He was made to be sin. In like manner, you are not righteous because you practice righteousness. You are righteous because you were *made* to be righteous.

Perhaps you are thinking, *Yes, I have been robed in the righteousness of Jesus Christ. He has clothed me in His right-standing with the Father.* That's a great concept—but it's a little weak. The sacrifice of the Son of God secured far more for us than new apparel. Redemption is about total regeneration. We dare not water down this principle to appease those who are satisfied with their limited understanding of the atoning work of Jesus Christ!

Now don't spill your coffee when you read the next few paragraphs. Your righteousness is predicated upon the fact that Jesus was made to be sin. If you weren't really *made righteous*, then Jesus was never *made to be sin*, and the whole truth of redemption is in jeopardy. You cannot have one without the other!

Furthermore, it seems to me that to the *degree* He was made sin, you were made righteous. Jesus did not just bear the politically correct sins of the world. He was made to be every heinous sin that ever crossed the perverted mind of fallen man. As disturbing as it may seem, He carried the sins of rape, incest and infanticide to the cross. Although His flesh must have cried out in revulsion, Jesus willingly allowed the vilest of sin to be placed upon Him in His suffering. While hanging on the cross, this pure Man who never committed one single sin suddenly felt the overwhelming pressure of the depraved nature of sin. He carried the past, present and future sins of man with Him to the cross, nailing them to the tree, securing eternal freedom for those who put their trust in Him.

The reason why I need to emphasize this point so strongly is in order for you to see the degree to which He was made to be sin. To the degree He was made sin, you were made righteous. You were not just made righteous in a superficial, inconsequential way; you were made righteous in every deep and lasting way that counts with the Father.

This is the theological principle of substitution at work here. Jesus became the substitutionary lamb, taking the place of sinful man at the judgment bar of Calvary. In His crucifixion we see the ultimate expression of the Old Testament picture of the scapegoat.

Under the Old Covenant, through the leadership of Moses, God revealed an incredible opportunity for the Israelites to experience atonement for their sins. According to Leviticus 16, Aaron (the high priest) was required by God to do four things in order to make atonement for Israel's iniquities and sins. (See Leviticus 16:20–22.) He was instructed:

- To take a "scapegoat" to the edge of the camp
- To lay his hands upon the animal
- To recite the sins of Israel
- To release the goat outside the camp

Unfortunately, this was only a limited atonement, because the entire process had to be repeated the following year.

This limited atonement was a foreshadow of the everlasting atonement, which was secured by the "eternal sacrifice" of the Lord Jesus Christ. Even as Aaron "put" the iniquities and sins on the head of this "scapegoat," the Father also "laid" the sins of the world upon the "head" of this sinless Lamb. (See Isaiah 53:4; Hebrews 9:28.) Jesus was the Lamb who was sent "outside the camp" bearing our reproach (Heb. 13:12).

Who Is Your Source?

GOD'S DESIRE IS for us to become an extension of His life through a dependent relationship with Him. New Covenant righteousness is about our dependence upon the Father to keep our righteousness secure through His covenant with the Son. Our righteousness is not based upon our good works—it is based upon the covenant held between the Father and the Son. As we share in the life of the Son, we are entitled to the same measure of righteousness that He secured through His perfect obedience to the Law of Moses! This dependence will lead to righteous acts of obedience, but the *source* is our relationship with the Father—not our good works. Our *doing* flows from our *being*. The new creation does the works of righteousness because he *has been made* righteous, not in order *to become* righteous! Who we are at the core of our essential identity determines how we respond to the biblical principles of submission and obedience.

Why did Jesus experience the abundant life in His thirty-three years on earth? It was because He understood the secret of absolute dependence upon the Father. The key to His victorious life and supernatural ministry was not His dependence upon His own personal deity. Oh yes, He was and is fully God. The fullness of the Godhead lived bodily in Him, and yet He commonly referred to Himself as the "Son of Man." And as such, He revealed the pattern for living.

As the Son of God, Jesus was the source of all creation and sustaining life. As the Son of God, He needed no one to sustain Him during His earthly sojourn. And yet as the Son of Man, he was completely dependent upon the Father to nourish Him with the life of heaven. That's why He boldly declared, "I can of Mine own self do nothing!" (See John 8:28.)

Astonishingly, Jesus never performed miracles as a divine being. He performed them as a mere man anointed by God. Acts 10:38 reveals His dependence upon the anointing: "How God anointed Jesus of Nazareth with the Holy Spirit and with power, who went about doing good and healing all who were oppressed by the devil, for God was with Him." Jesus needed the anointing in order to perform the miraculous! In addition to serving the needs of suffering humanity through healing the sick, Jesus was also showing the master key to life and righteousness, which is total dependence upon the Father.

ERASER MAN

SEVERAL YEARS AGO while standing in a ticket line at the local cinema, my eyes were drawn to a life-size cardboard cutout of Arnold Schwarzenegger advertising his latest motion picture. Larger than life, with bulging biceps and a steely determination in his eyes, Arnold struck terror in the hearts of the lawless, while the caption proclaimed the title and theme of the movie. *"Eraser: He will erase your past to protect your future."*

Suddenly, in a moment of inspiration I recounted that this is exactly what Jesus Christ offers to us through the completed work of redemption and the formation of the new creation. You see, the intended result of the new birth experience is not just to separate us from the deformity of sin, but to re-form us in the image of righteousness.

I believe that the church has majored on behavior modification when we should focus on identity revelation. When you begin to live in the reality of whom you were made to be in Christ Jesus, then even hell itself cannot stop you. When you fully awaken to righteousness, then sickness and disease cannot destroy you, discouragement cannot abort your purpose and poverty can no longer hold you captive. When you surrendered your life to Christ, you were immediately brought into right standing with God because of the sacrifice of the spotless Lamb. You must believe it! Lay claim to it! Boldly confess it! Then you will begin to manifest the reality of it. *Jesus Christ has erased your past in order to protect your future.*

Christian growth is the process of becoming who you already are.

Six

BECOMING WHO
YOU ALREADY ARE

M ILLIONS OF PEOPLE are born again by the will of God and have the right to become fully matured sons, but they never go on to maturity because they lack a proper understanding of their essential identity in Christ. Our spiritual perception always determines our final destination. If we perceive the new birth experience to be the final destination in life, then we will settle for something less than our full potential in the kingdom of God.

> Behold, what manner of love the Father hath bestowed upon us, that we should be called the sons

of God: therefore the world knoweth us not, because it knew him not. Beloved, *now* are we the sons of God, and it doth not yet appear what we shall be: but we know that, when he shall appear, we shall be like him; for we shall see him as he is.

—1 JOHN 3:1–2, KJV, EMPHASIS ADDED

It is hard to avoid the noticeable tension between these two phrases: "*now* are we the sons of God" and "it doth *not yet* appear." John is showing us that our *identity* is a settled fact, but our spiritual *maturity* is yet to be determined. We are the sons of God on the journey to becoming fully matured. Anyone who has ever parented children will tell you that there is a vast difference between an immature son and one who is fully developed in those things pertaining to his destiny.

The new birth experience is THE defining moment in a person's life. Prior to the new birth, we merely existed, "dead in our trespasses and sins." "But God, who is rich in mercy, because of His great love with which He loved us...made us alive together with Christ" (Eph. 2:4–5). Following the miracle of regeneration, there is nothing you can do to become any more of a son of God than what you have already done. You can become a *mature* son. You can become an *obedient* son. You can become a *faithful* son. But you are already a *son* of God.

Consider the process of being born to your physical parents for a moment. Your gender was determined at the moment of conception, and after nine months, your "flesh" birth revealed "what" you are for the doctor to see and your parents to celebrate. You were genetically constructed as a male or female; there is no "in between" category. Now throughout the whole of your life you can choose educational, emotional and physical activities that will enhance your "maleness" or your "femininity," but there is no activity that will alter your *essential* identity. Your essential identity was determined by God, programmed into your genes and revealed at birth. It is not a matter of your physical attributes as much as it is the reflection of your inner man.

Let me explain another way. Working out three times each week at a health club may make me a strong man, but I am already male. Completing my Ph.D. may make me an educated man, but I am already male. Likewise, you may enhance and develop your identity as a son of God, but you are already a son! And there is nothing you can do to make you any more of a son (after the new birth) than what you have already done.

Many Christians are engaged in a life-or-death struggle to become who they already are in Christ. Instead of perceiving the reality of their new identity, they continue the search to discover the very thing they have already become. When I speak of becoming who you already are, I am describing the process by which you come to terms with who you are in Christ. This essential identity was clearly defined in the mind of God long before the ages began. How do we know this to be true? Because what God planned for your life to become was charted out in the mystery of His Son long before He stepped out of eternity and into time.

Robert McGee speaks directly to this issue when he writes:

> Perhaps we wish that during regeneration God had turned us purple or perhaps given us yellow spots. At least then we would see a difference in ourselves. However, God has gone to the trouble of communicating that He has made us brand-new inside. And now it's up to us to take Him at His Word.[1]

The Image Maker has already deposited everything in you, through His incorruptible seed, that you will ever need to become who you already are in Christ. This incorruptible seed lives and abides within us, continually growing and bearing eternal fruit. Second Peter 1:3 says, "According as his divine power hath given unto us all things that pertain unto life and godliness..." (KJV). What do you presently need to be confident in your essential identity? What do you need to succeed in overcoming every challenge to your destiny? The answer is already within you! The key to your success in life is contained in the seed of God's incorruptible Word, which exists within your spirit.

I find J. B. Phillips' translation of 1 Peter 1:23 fascinating: "For you are not just mortals now but sons of God; the live, permanent Word of the living God has given you his own indestructible heredity." His own indestructible heredity is within us. The seed of an exchanged life is within us; the solution is within us. There is life-giving hope within us.

Have you ever stopped to realize that the only aspect of creation that struggles with its identity is mankind? The birds, bees, dogs and fleas do not give the issue of identity a second thought. Have you ever observed an apple sapling struggling with an identity crisis, desperate to become an apple tree? Certainly not! The genetic structure of that apple tree—roots, trunk, sap, leaves and branches—are all destined for one thing, and it knows it. That one thing is to produce fruit after its own kind. The destiny is in the seed. The "guidance system" of the genetic structure relieves the plant kingdom, as well as the whole of creation, from stressing over being something "other" than what it really is! With the exception of mankind, God's entire kingdom is at peace with its inherent design and ultimate destiny.

The prophet Jeremiah heard the cry of the Father's heart and recorded His plea when He said, "My dear people, observe the homing instincts of geese, storks, swallows and pigeons. Will you likewise recognize your need to belong, and return to Me—your true home of freedom?" (Jer. 8:7).[2]

GROWING INTO YOUR IDENTITY

CHRISTIAN GROWTH IS the process of becoming who we already are in Christ. The destination for your life in the kingdom of God (in this present age) is to be conformed into the image of Christ and to grow up into Him in all things. The Image Maker desires for us to continue growing spiritually, until we reach maturity and are functioning as the fully developed Son. This journey is not complete in our lives until the world cannot tell the difference between the Jesus of the Bible and His ongoing incarnated body. The destination has not been reached until the line between us and Jesus becomes indivisible, until we live like Jesus, talk like Jesus, respond like Jesus and love like Jesus.

The wonderful thing about this "becoming process" is that we have all of God's grace at our disposal. In Romans 4 we discover that Abraham was first "named" father and then "became" a father because he dared to trust God to do what only God could do—raise the dead to life; with a word make something out of nothing. Because God "named" us the new creation, we have all the grace to manifest new creation realities—personally, prophetically, practically. We are all on a journey...some hammering out the dreadful duty of self-denial, attempting to *manufacture* a life in Christ, whereas others *live* in the awe of a magnificent obsession to simply become who they already are.

Now after considering the importance of this principle, the immediate question that springs to mind is this: Why does the Father call us to spiritual maturity? After all, if getting to heaven is the only thing that matters, then why grow up? Why spend so much of our time praying and studying the Word of God if it produces no personal profit? Who wants to suffer through unnecessary growing pains? I believe that those questions reveal the crux of the matter. The primary reason why so many people say the sinner's prayer, walk away from the altar and never go on to discipleship is because they have never been shown the value of growing up into Christ in all things.

There are many reasons we have been called to grow spiritually, but the foremost reason is this: Only the fully matured son can inherit everything the Father has willed to him. Until the time of our maturity we are kept under tutors, and our inheritance is held "in trust." And only as we mature is our inheritance gradually released unto us. Upon full maturity we then qualify to receive the fullness of our inheritance. Romans 8:14 declares, "For as many as are led by the Spirit of God, these are sons [the fully matured sons] of God." So the goal of the Holy Spirit is to prepare you for your spiritual inheritance.

Whether your mission is touching individuals or multitudes, changing communities or diapers, planning cities or evening meals, redeeming nations or grocery coupons, reforming social structures or structuring your child's homework, you need the wisdom of maturity in order to reach your destination. Whether you're leading Cub Scouts or a congregation, you need to be led by the Spirit of God. The sufficiently matured son qualifies for the fullness of his inheritance.

BECOMING THROUGH CHASTENING

THE MOST FRUSTRATING words I ever heard spoken as a child were these: "Son, this is going to hurt me worse than it hurts you." I knew that pronouncement was going to be followed by my father's "placing the board of education on my seat of knowledge for the purpose of applied learning." The frustration I experienced was on two levels, one physical and the other philosophical. I could not see how this process hurt him more than it did me. As a father, I now understand.

The writer of Hebrews writes these shocking words:

> "My son, do not despise the chastening of the LORD, nor be discouraged when you are rebuked by Him; for whom the LORD loves He chastens, and scourges every son whom He receives." If you endure chastening, God deals with you as with sons; for what son is there whom a father does not chasten? But if you are without chastening, of which all have become partakers, then you are illegitimate, and not sons.
>
> —HEBREWS 12:5–8

Even the chastening process of the Lord is for our spiritual development. But when rejection is present in our lives, it makes *correction* seem like *destruction*. The corrective process of the kingdom may hurt your "flesh," but it will not destroy your purpose. God is intent on developing a son, not destroying an enemy.

I believe that the devil works to alienate us from the corrective process of the kingdom by sowing seeds of mistrust in our lives. I have ministered to many Christians who do not trust The Image Maker's intention in divine correction, because they have been abused by human authority figures. Not recognizing how they have been "set up" by the devil, they despise the chastening of the Lord. Consequently, they never mature as a son and cannot be given their inheritance in the kingdom.

TRANSMITTING THE IMAGE

ALTHOUGH THE NEW birth experience formed the new creation deep within us, restoring us back into the likeness of The Image Maker, the challenge we encounter is in communicating (or transmitting) that new image back to our minds, will and emotions.

The transmission of these new creation realities is a continual process in life. This co-venture is between you and the Holy Spirit with the Word of God serving as the instruction manual. He supplies the grace; you cooperate by supplying the faith. He supplies the power, but you must make available the vessel. He provides the wisdom; you develop the understanding.

In his book *In Christ*, A. J. Gordon writes this striking statement: "Thus Christ, in taking up man into Himself, takes all that belongs to him. Instead of rending him away from his natural connections, He embraces all these with him in Himself, that He might sanctify them all."[3]

Let me show you just where this process of growing and maturing begins. It's very simple, so don't miss the subtle truth while looking for complexities.

REVELATION PRODUCES REVOLUTION

As WE RACE along the information superhighway of the early twenty-first century, it is absolutely necessary that we become "renewed in the spirit of our minds." Renewing our minds to the knowledge of our identity in Christ takes more than factual information; it necessitates spiritual revelation.

Proverbs 23:7 declares that "as [a man] thinks in his heart, so is he." Long before that familiar line worked its way into Psychology 101, the Bible identified it as being a spiritual principle. The true secret to living the new creation life is to begin renewing our minds to new creation realities. It's really a matter of programming our minds with the revelation that will ultimately set us free. Watch this carefully—information will not set you free, but revelation will.

What many Christians have failed to discern is that there is a vast difference between truth and revelation. Let me explain it to you like this. Truth doesn't require a personal application to be true, but revelation cannot exist independently of a personal application. Revelation is actually the truth that I have received *and* applied.

For instance: In his groundbreaking book *Atom: The Journey Across the Subatomic Cosmos*, Isaac Asimov teaches us that:

> Just as a fission produces a flood of antineutrinos because of the numerous conversions of neutrons to protons it makes necessary, so fusion produces a flood of neutrinos because of equally massive conversions of the same two particles. In the fusion of hydrogen to helium, for instance, four hydrogen nuclei, made up of four protons altogether, are converted into one helium nucleus made up of two protons and two neutrons. In the process, two positrons are formed, and with the positrons, two neutrinos.[4]

That statement is true according to the law of quantum physics, but it certainly isn't revelation to most of us! So, there is a difference between truth and revelation.

In John 8:31 Jesus said, "If you abide in My word, you are My disciples indeed." Following that commission, He continued on to say, "And you shall know the truth, and the truth shall make you free." For that matter, *truth* will not set you free, but *revelation* will! (I can almost hear your gasp as you read that last sentence.) It is the truth that has gone on to become revelation through a personal application that makes us free. Only the truth that we hear, believe, receive and apply will set us free.

Many of you reading this book desperately want to change the broken areas of your lives, but you are going about it all wrong. Perhaps you want to heal a broken marriage or spark a dying career or kick a bad habit, and you are frustrated with yourself because you feel powerless to change. You have deceived yourself into thinking that one morning you'll wake up and everything will be magically changed. Wrong! Before your situation will ever change, *you* may have to change. And sometimes change only comes through the process of spiritual conflict.

When paraphrasing John 8:31, the Jerusalem Bible says, "Your mind must be renewed by a spiritual revolution." Do you know what the object of a revolution is? The purpose of a revolution is to overthrow "governmental authority." If your mind has been ruled by the "governmental authority" of the kingdom of darkness, you can dethrone its power by renewing your mind to the truth of God's Word.

CASTING DOWN THE WRONG IMAGE

IN ANCIENT DAYS, cities were built within massive walls, thereby protecting their citizens. When they were under siege from an opposing army, the wall provided a formidable barrier that protected the city, holding the enemy at bay. Before any enemy force could expect to conquer a city, it first had to overcome that protective shield.

In addition to almost indestructible walls, towers were erected in strategic places throughout the city. During times of battle, warriors would position themselves in these stations, which towered above the surrounding wall. From these high vantage points they could see the location of the advancing troops and plan their strategy of defense and counterattack.

In order for the enemy to take the city, three objectives had to be accomplished. First, the wall had to be scaled or penetrated. Second, the towers had to be invaded. Third, the men of military strategy had to be captured. After the military leaders were captured or killed, then the general army was left without direction. Such was the strategy for first-century battles.

In 2 Corinthians 10, we see this very principle illustrated—not in a city, but in a mind. Originally our minds were enemy-held territories. Our minds were the base of operation for the powers of this world. Rebellion, anger, lust, insecurity, intimidation and rejection ruled without resistance. These forces of darkness had complete control over our lives through our minds. That's why Paul uses military words and ideas that suggest physical combat, even though everything being described here occurs in the mind.

> For though we walk in the flesh, we do not war after the flesh: (For the weapons of our warfare are not carnal, but mighty through God to the pulling down of strong holds;) casting down imaginations, and every high thing that exalteth itself against the knowledge of God, and bringing into captivity every thought to the obedience of Christ.
>
> —2 CORINTHIANS 10:3–5, KJV

Most Christians are familiar with these verses, but not the context from which they are taken. Rather than being a passage on the importance of spiritual warfare, the real issue at stake here is Paul's identity as an apostle of the Lord Jesus Christ. His authority as a New Testament apostle flows out of his identity as the new creation. Always remember the principle found here. *You will never discover your true authority until you first discover your true identity.*

Although the light of the glorious gospel has set us free, the enemy still attempts to operate through the strongholds that he has established. He seeks to rule our lives through the habits we established when we were under his

109

control. The real battleground is at the point of the stronghold—the thing that we fall back under when pressure comes upon us. In a moment of pressure, many Christians still hide under the stronghold of personal addiction. They bow their knees to the ruling power of gluttony, alcohol, nicotine, sex, anger, withdrawal and so forth because they do not know who they really are. In order to change effectively the behavior, we have to cast down the imagination and bring our thoughts captive to the image of Christ.

A DANGEROUS MISUNDERSTANDING

INHERENT WITHIN YOUR essential identity exists the capacity to behave accordingly. If you do not understand your identity as a son or daughter of the kingdom, then you will live your entire life beneath the privileges of your sonship. Do you know who you are? Do you fully perceive whom God made you to be in Christ Jesus?

I once read a story about a mother who lived in a rural community. One day she returned from the local grocery store and discovered her six children in the backyard huddled around something interesting. Although she was at a distance, she could tell by their body language that they were totally absorbed in their discovery.

As she watched, she suddenly discovered the source of their excitement. Six baby skunks had wandered into their yard from the woods, and the children had them surrounded. Unaware of the imminent danger, the children were fascinated by these cute little furry critters.

Immediately recognizing the potential found in these little "stinkers," their mother screamed, "Run, children, run!" Hearing the panic in their mother's voice, each child grabbed a skunk and scurried away from the invisible danger. Misunderstandings can be dangerous.

Destroying What He Did Not Understand

After a recent medical checkup, I stepped out of the doctor's office and back into the waiting room to verify my insurance information before leaving the building. I found myself standing behind a young lady and her father who were also there for the very same purpose. When I walked up behind them, I could feel the tension in the room. As the young lady desperately rummaged through her purse trying to find her insurance card, I could literally see the back of her father's neck turning purple with rage. Then he suddenly exploded with anger. "You are so stupid!" he chided her. "I have never seen anyone as worthless as you! I should have given you away years ago!"

In his rage the man grabbed his daughter by the arm and jerked her out of the line. As they stepped aside, I could see that she had Down's syndrome. With tears in her eyes, she continued rummaging through her purse without even responding to his cruel, biting words.

Trembling with anger, I stepped up to the counter and shoved my hand deep into my pocket for my insurance card, only to discover that I had forgotten it and left it in the car. For a moment, I couldn't decide whether to go after my card or turn around and punch this heartless savage in the mouth. Suddenly I had an idea.

Turning my body slightly, so that I was facing him, I spoke loudly to the receptionist. "Excuse me, ma'am, it seems that I have forgotten my insurance card as well. I am not an idiot. I am not worthless. Like this young lady, I have simply made a mistake. As a matter of fact, I am probably far more educated than this man who is verbally abusing his daughter."

The room suddenly went so silent you could have heard a pin drop. The man hung his head in embarrassment and almost ran for the door in his haste to get out of the office.

After he left, the receptionist and the office staff broke out into applause. It seems this had happened before, and the nurses felt powerless to say anything lest they lose their jobs.

Whenever I think of that young lady, my heart breaks. I have often prayed for her protection and the deliverance of her demonized father. Unfortunately, she is not alone in her pain, as many others are subjected to the same degree of abuse that she has experienced. Evidently, her handicap had blinded her father to her intrinsic worth as a human being, and she suffered as a result of his ignorance.

"When the purpose of a thing is not understood, abuse is inevitable," writes Myles Munroe.[5] An honest assessment of most of our lives would prove this to be true. Even though we may not be prone to fits of rage and torrential verbal abuse, we often devalue others with our unkind, inconsiderate words. We must learn to value those things The Image Maker values, and human life is at the top of His personal list.

Now that we have seen a glimpse into The Image Maker's desire for us to become who we already are in Christ, I want us to open our eyes to the unveiling of our essential identity.

Buried beneath the layers of rejection,
abandonment, misunderstanding
and spiritual ignorance is the person
God created you to be.

Seven

UNVEILING YOUR
ESSENTIAL IDENTITY

W ITH A BIBLE school diploma carefully filed away, and a fire burning in his heart, my father cautiously navigated the moving truck through the traffic of St. Paul/Minneapolis as we began the journey toward the Black Hills of South Dakota. Eyes wide open, taking in all of the scenery, I sat perched on the edge of the seat, firing every question my four-year-old mind could conceive. "Are there cowboys and Indians living in the hills? Do the deer and the antelope really play, like the song says? Where will you work, Daddy? What will we name the new church?"

At twenty-four years of age, my father was called to plant a church in a state we had never visited and a town with a name I could barely pronounce. The task would not be as easy as we hoped. As a bivocational pastor, his days were spent working in the world's largest gold mine, while his nights were filled discipling new converts in Sturgis, South Dakota.

Almost thirty years later, I visited that same gold mine on a summer vacation with my wife and three sons. As we sat in the parking lot watching the miners exit the shafts after finishing their evening shift, I was shocked to discover how inaccurate my memory actually was. The illusions of excitement, intrigue and glamour were shattered before my eyes. The men exiting the mine were dirty, exhausted and happy to be off work for another evening. This was not *Romancing the Stone*. Mining gold is hard work, requiring extraordinary strength, incredible energy and a commitment to continue working even when you do not immediately see the reward of your labor.

In much the same way, the process of unveiling your essential identity is like that of a gold miner blasting through the hard shell of the surface and sifting through tons of crushed stone just to discover that one precious ounce of pure gold. Buried beneath the layers of rejection, abandonment, misunderstanding and spiritual ignorance is the person God created you to be. The reward is well worth the effort.

MINING FOR GOLD

ANYTHING WORTH HAVING is worth mining for. Like a land surveyor who determines the value of property based upon what he can see without giving consideration to the rich deposit lying beneath the surface, many people determine their self-worth by the landscape of their lives. Comparing the surface of their lives with the landscape of those around them, they never give consideration to the mineral deposit hidden deep beneath the obvious deficiencies with which they struggle.

Have you ever been perplexed by a loved one's lack of confidence, the evidence of weakness in someone's understanding of self-worth? Have you ever asked yourself any of the following questions?

- Why is my husband so indecisive when it comes to decisions that directly affect the future of our marriage and family?

- Why does my friend constantly compare herself with those around her?

- Why are my children so driven toward personal achievement, even at the expense of their family life?

- Why does my supervisor find it so difficult to be honest with her mistakes and ask for forgiveness?

- Why are my associates afraid of failing and yet also afraid of succeeding?

- Why is my best friend so preoccupied with his past failures?

- Why is my loved one so passive about everything in life?

- Why can't my wife relax? Why is she driven toward having everything in our lives perfect?

Each of the questions reveals a lack of understanding of that person's identity. Many of us have never been taught the skills necessary to mine the gold found at the core of our identities. As long as we are blind to our self-worth, we will never discover the priceless qualities that have been deposited deep within our spirits. Unveiling our essential identity is a process, not an event.

This process begins when we understand the power inherent within our self-worth. Our self-worth determines our ability to give and receive love. Our self-worth determines our ability to recognize value in those who are around us. Either consciously or subconsciously, our self-worth sets the agenda for our marriages, careers, personal accomplishment and individual fulfillment in life.

When we fail to accept ourselves as image bearers of the infinite Creator, we find it increasingly difficult to accept others, as a young man and his beautiful wife discovered many years ago.

THINGS ARE NOT AS THEY SEEM

SHE WAS AS talented as she was attractive. Loved by her family, admired by her friends and respected by those to whom she had ministered, this young lady had a bright future before her.

With her love for people, she was always busy helping others. As the daughter of a pastor, there was no shortage of opportunities to serve the Lord by caring for people. Her evenings and weekends were filled ministering to inner-city children and assisting invalids. Many nights she gave up her bed to accommodate those unexpected visitors who dropped in for a few days of pastoral care and good old Southern hospitality. But in spite of this young lady's obvious qualities of compassion, selflessness and long-suffering, she harbored a deep personal secret. She did not really feel accepted.

When she was seventeen years old, her world came crashing down. Choosing truth over popularity, her father confessed to an affair and began the process of rebuilding his life with integrity and righteousness. The rejection in her life intensified, resulting in a sense of betrayal and abandonment.

As she grew and developed as a teenager, the search for acceptance led her into an unhealthy dating relationship that ended in a disastrous breakup. The relationship gave way to shame, and shame to rebellion.

Determined to bury the past and create a new self-image, she went to college. During her freshman year, she fell in love with a young man who appeared to have it all together. He projected confidence, purpose and seemed deeply committed to the same values she held dear. Their whirlwind romance found them married within seven months of meeting.

It didn't take long for her to discover that his carefully constructed persona masked deep fears and insecurity. He was brash, domineering and controlling. More concerned with getting his personal needs met, he neglected her and at times even rejected her. The insecurity grew like cancer deep within her soul until finally it metastasized into bitterness. They were unprepared to live together according to wisdom.

His personal ambition quickly found a place of opportunity, and within a relatively short period of time, he was serving as the senior pastor of a small but growing church in an upwardly mobile community. Plunging himself deeply into the responsibilities of pastoring along with the opportunity to expand into international travel, he was consumed with the desire to succeed. He worked as if he were trying to prove something to himself or to someone else.

After four years of marriage, both began to realize the irrevocable damage that had been done to one another. They decided they could not continue on the same path of destruction any longer. Even though their love for one another was strong, their insecurities made it difficult to care for one another.

That young couple was Judith and I in the early years of our marriage. At that time, we had a number of critical choices to make. Would I love Judith and accept her even when she did not make the choices I would make? Would Judith love me during my journey to break the hardened soil of my heart to discover gentleness, goodness and long-suffering? The choices were real. The decisions were tough. The nights were long as the wounds were probed and repentance was sought. Fortunately, we turned to the grace of God and began the journey toward wholeness.

As we look back on those days of self-inflicted pain, we believe they were among the most important days in our marriage. Even before we were married, the patterns were laid for rejection and insecurity. As Judith's insecurity intensified, I responded in the worst way possible, by threatening further rejection. As she withdrew, my fear of failure and abandonment intensified.

Through the process of wounding one another, we discovered the critical importance of taking accountability for our individual attitudes. One of the hardest lessons for me to learn was that I am responsible for my responses, regardless of the provocation.

As we sought the wisdom of God, we began to see how our individual self-worth either crippled or completed our marriage relationship.

Enemies of Your Essential Identity

1. Lack of revelation

Ask yourself the question, "Who has the right to define me?" In the presence of insecurity, *someone* or *something* will arise with an agenda to define your life. It may be as general as a self-centered culture or as specific as misguided authority figures, but someone or something will label you. I am convinced that the Word of God, applied through the wisdom of the Holy Spirit, is the only thing that has a right—and is capable—of defining you. But you will never discover your essential identity unless you have eyes to see and ears to hear.

This is the difference between touring the gold mine and working in the gold mine. The difference between a tourist and a qualified miner is this. One has never had his eyes opened, and the other cannot avoid seeing what is undeniably clear. A tourist never sees what a qualified geologist cannot ignore.

In these terms, the Pharisees were the tourists while the disciples were in the process of becoming qualified geologists. In other words, the Pharisees listened with a predetermined disposition toward the words of Jesus, but the disciples were willing to give everything away in order to gain what they could not see. One listened as an instructor while the other listened as a learner.

Granted, it is much easier to wander aimlessly through life without giving any consideration to whether or not you are living in the reality of your essential identity. It is always easier to assume the identity of another than it is to become yourself.

Far too many Christians buy books and tapes because of the personality who authored them, not for the information they contain. They attend seminars and conferences for superficial reasons, not internal ones. These are the people who focus on outer image at the expense of inner image. They settle for less than they were created to be.

2. Generational curses

One of the foremost ways that strongholds of insecurity and rejection are established in people's lives is by the spiritual transfer of the sins of the fathers unto the children.

It is not unusual to discover that a child suffering with a distorted self-image is the product of one or both parents who struggled with the very same malaise.

I do not believe this is simply the product of environmental influence as some pop-psychologists would lead you to believe. Interestingly, I have ministered to a number of people who were separated from their parents at birth, only to be reunited later in their life and to discover that they were exhibiting the very same character traits as their parents.

In his book *Freedom From Guilt*, Bruce Narramore gives two examples of how strongholds, both positive and negative, are passed down generationally. He first traced the descendants of Jonathan Edwards, a fiery American colonial preacher and theologian. Of the 374 descendants tracked, 100 became ministers or missionaries; 100 became professors; 100 were lawyers and judges; 60 were doctors; and 14 were college presidents.

The second man was a convicted criminal named Max Jukes. Of the 917 descendants studied, there were 130 convicted criminals; 310 professional paupers; 400 who were seriously injured or who physically degenerated due to their lifestyles; 60 habitual thieves or pickpockets; and 17 murderers. In the entire group of 917 descendants studied, only 20 learned a trade, and 10 of those were taught this trade while in prison.[1]

The unveiling of your essential identity can be hindered because of unresolved issues lurking in the past. Satan operates from the past, while God works from the future. It has been said that the only person whose problems are all behind him is probably a school bus driver. A man will deal with his children exactly as he was dealt with unless he makes a conscious choice to do otherwise. This process will continue generation after generation until the curse is realized and broken through repentance and prayer.

3. Wrong relationships

The most powerful force in the universe, outside of God, is human relationships. Your relationships are the key to your personal success or failure; they will either coach you into destiny or restrict you from your ultimate purpose. Everything that we are today, good and bad, is a product of the people we know and the lessons we've learned.

Let me share a couple of examples of wrong relationships. You may be attending a church to which God did not lead you. You may be working in a company that is not conducive to your spiritual health. You may be dating an unbeliever. You may be in business with someone who refuses to honor your value system. These are examples of types of relationships that hold the potential to hinder your spiritual growth and maturity.

Wrong relationships are not always comprised of evil people. Many times they are good people trapped in relationships that are simply not right... for them. I have met people who have joined a church because they were attracted to a program, a musical style or the children's ministry, not because the Father had set them there. When they finally realized they were in the wrong place, they began looking for carnal reasons to justify their departure. Rather than seeking the will of God, they began looking for failures in the church leadership in order to give them a reason for leaving.

Relationships are complex—they have both static and dynamic aspects associated with them. While certain covenant relationships *are* forever, those people within the relationship are in the process of growing and evolving into whom they were created to be. I counseled a man several years ago who had a very specific list of the qualities he was looking for in a spouse. As a very accomplished professional who had dedicated his entire life to achieving his career goals, he was committed to finding the ideal woman. After looking at his list, it dawned on me that the woman he was looking for would serve as a model wife *today* but would fill the role of a daughter *tomorrow*. In other words, as he grew older and his needs changed, he needed a wife who would grow with him rather than an ideal image stuck in the past.

After seventeen years of marriage, my needs have changed. What I needed as an eighteen-year-old boy is far different from what I need as a thirty-five-year-old man. What my wife presently needs as a mature woman is far different from what she needed as a young girl. Thankfully, we committed to a journey, not an event. As we become clearer on who we are individually, we have learned to respond positively to each other's growth rather than reacting in fear.

4. Insecurity

A feeling of insecurity is based upon an inner belief of personal inadequacy. In our desire for acceptance, we often find ourselves falling short of others' expectations for us, which leaves us feeling insecure about our ability to measure up.

I am convinced that much of the insecurity with which we struggle is not a result of who we are (or who we are not), but rather a result of using a false measuring stick to determine our worth and value. We often fall into the trap of comparing ourselves with those whom we perceive to be "perfect" in those ways in which we desire to excel, and in doing so we block the wisdom of God from revealing our life's purpose. Paul said:

> For we dare not make ourselves of the number, or compare ourselves with some that commend themselves: but they measuring themselves by themselves, and

comparing themselves among themselves, are not wise.
—2 Corinthians 10:12, kjv

The real danger in comparing ourselves with one another is that we develop the tendency to settle for the lowest common denominator. If I allow my father to become the benchmark for my destiny, then once I have reached his status, I will consider myself as having apprehended the ultimate purpose for my life. In accepting someone else's destiny as the pattern for my life, I have blocked the wisdom of God from revealing my high calling. In comparing myself with someone else, I have prevented God from revealing my identity. The measuring stick for your destiny is not your husband, wife, brother, sister or classmate; it is the divine pattern established by The Image Maker.

Idealism is the driving force behind insecurity. When people are not grounded in truth and reality, they often find themselves striving to become something beyond the realm of their purpose in life. Struggling to become the ideal mother, passionate lover, gourmet chef, child psychologist, witty conversationalist, aggressive businesswoman, loving daughter, loyal friend or gorgeous supermodel, most women find themselves buried under a mountain of despair. Instead of accepting the divine design for their lives, they have allowed society to superimpose an image of the "ideal" woman on them. I'm sure you've seen her in many of the commercials on television.

She wakes up every morning with her makeup perfectly applied and her breath as fresh as a cool mountain breeze. Throughout the day, she has the perfect answer to every question asked by a runny-nosed three-year-old or a middle-aged man suffering midlife crisis. (Actually there really isn't much difference between the two!) She works all day like a team of highly trained sled dogs, and she still has the energy to attend her favorite charity function—every night of the week! She is completely capable of eating an entire side of beef without gaining a single ounce and has never found herself in an awkward social situation for which she was not prepared. She's better than a Proverbs 31 woman—she is the Proverbs 32 woman!

I have just one question for you: Where do they get these people? It is quite obvious that they do not exist in the real world.

In his insightful work, *The Search for Significance*, Robert McGee writes:

> Our self-concept is determined not only by how we view ourselves but by how we think others perceive us. Basing our self-worth on what we believe others think of us causes us to become addicted to their approval.[2]

Those people who struggle with insecurity often suffer emotionally, in addition to the toll it takes on their relational, physical and spiritual lives. Striving to gain the approval of others, they usually end up with arrested emotional development, which aborts the unveiling of their essential identity.

5. Rejection

Fear is the guardian of rejection. Wherever you find rejection present, you will find fear inviting, reinforcing and protecting it. That's why when Adam sinned, his first response to God was, "I heard You coming, and I was afraid!"

"Afraid of what?" you ask. After all, Adam had never seen the wrath of God. He was totally unfamiliar with any form of anger or judgment. Like a tropical flower in a greenhouse, Adam had been in a loving, caring, nurturing environment since the day he was created. And yet he was still afraid of rejection. Man's greatest fear is that he will not be received, respected and loved.

Unveiling Your Essential Identity

For six thousand years mankind has sought to regain the feeling of security, self-worth and unconditional acceptance we experienced originally in the Garden. We search for significance in materialism, sexual gratification, achievement, self-improvement and even religion. But none of it seems to work, because this is a spiritual problem, and a spiritual problem cannot be solved with a natural solution.

Most all of us fear rejection in some form or another. Even though we take great care to protect our emotions by telling ourselves that it really doesn't matter, we still fall prey to its devastating effect time and again. Quite frankly, it is just as easy to shut your ears to your native language as it is to ignore rejection. Since rejection is a form of communication, we cannot ignore it, but we can learn to respond to it.

As a matter of fact, most of us have learned to handle the more extreme forms of rejection. Imagine yourself driving down the street, humming to your favorite tune on the radio, semiaware of the other drivers around you as you inadvertently change lanes without signaling. As you timidly look in your rearview mirror, you see the red face of an enraged driver behind you, cursing you in three different languages. Finally, he pulls up next to you at the stoplight, rolls down his window and shouts, "Hey, stupid, get a real driver's license next time!"

Now as embarrassing as that situation may be, it has very little effect on you beyond a few minutes of emotional discomfort. Why? There are two reasons. First of all, the rejection came from some unknown individual who had absolutely no influence in your life or authority over you. Second, the form of rejection was so obvious, intense and typical of most drivers on the road today that it has almost no effect on our lives.

Now contrast that driving mishap with other forms of

127

rejection, which seem to have significant impact upon our ability to retain self-worth. Consider your reaction when you were told by the third-grade teacher you loved and admired, "You will never learn to spell correctly!" How do you feel when you receive a disgusted look from your wife or an impatient look from your employer? I have ministered to individuals whose lives were crushed by the words of a careless father who shouted, "You will never amount to anything!"

If this is really true, then why do we carry on the cycle of rejection from one generation to the next and from one relationship to another? Consider the insight offered by Robert S. McGee when he wrote:

> Rejection can be a very effective, though destructive, motivation. Without lifting a finger, we can send the message that our targeted individual doesn't meet our standards. We can harness this person's instinctive desire for acceptance until we have changed and adapted his or her behavior to suit our tastes and purposes. This is how rejection enables us to control the actions of another human being.[3]

The percentage of people who use rejection as a tool of manipulation is probably larger than we realize. This is a clear and present danger in both personal relationships and in larger social groups. Unfortunately, there are pastors who seem to specialize in manipulating people with a message that declares, "Obey, and you'll be accepted; disobey, and you'll be rejected!" Usually this message goes far beyond the basic commands of the Bible to include the culture of the church as well. We see the same pressure present wherever conformity is required, from politics to prison. Manipulation always distorts the unveiling of essential identity.

6. Unforgiveness

Unforgiveness is the most destructive force in the universe. When we allow unforgiveness access into our lives, we set in motion a chain of circumstances that often results in emotional, spiritual and relational destruction. Forgiveness is for the sake of the offended as much as it is for the offender.

Because there are many myths surrounding the issue of forgiveness, I want to help you to master the truth by examining three powerful truths.

To the degree that we are willing to forgive others, God will forgive us. It's a frightening fact to discover, but many times our attitudes toward one another predetermine God's attitude toward us. Our willingness to forgive men reveals the faithfulness of God.

Forgiveness does not always mean forgetting. True, the Bible does say that God forgives and forgets, but let's look at what I believe that verse really means. Speaking prophetically for God, Jeremiah says, "I will forgive their iniquity, and their sin I will remember no more" (Jer. 31:34). But that doesn't mean that God has forgotten in the same sense as if you were to forget where you placed your car keys. God doesn't suffer from amnesia. God forgives to the degree that He holds no resentment against us and refuses to condemn us based upon those sins of our past. God forgets to the degree that He feels about us the way that He would feel if He had amnesia.

There is such a thing as righteous remembering. Righteous remembering keeps a clear picture of the past but tempers it with grace and mercy. In fact, to the children of Israel, the Feast of Passover was to be a time of righteous remembrance. Not only were they instructed to remember the mercy of God, but they were also encouraged to remember their deliverance from the pain. The process of their redemption was as much a part of their remembrance as the ultimate liberation. The bondage itself wasn't memorialized, but the deliverance was. The monument was to the possibilities of the future, not the pain of the past. Redemptive remembering should always motivate us toward a better future; it should not tie us to a crippled past.

Oftentimes offenses continue to fester in relationships because acceptance takes the place of forgiveness. Most of us have learned how to "stuff" our hurt and go on without ever being honest with ourselves and with our pain. To deny the emotional pain in which you find yourself is to deny God's right to heal you. Until you learn to become honest with yourself, you will never be able to be honest with others.

Several years ago I found myself in a difficult situation. God was dealing with me about a relational challenge that had developed within my staff, and I was avoiding Him like the bubonic plague. He began reproving me with a gentle whisper that rapidly progressed to a loud shout, and still I shut Him out. Finally after several days of absolute misery, I surrendered to that wonderful compelling voice. (I would rather have God shout at me than ignore me!)

When I finally humbled myself and opened my ears to hear, this is what the Holy Spirit said, "Until you face it, you will never discover the grace to displace it." What sweet deliverance! The grace of God does not flow to nonexistent issues.

A wise man once said, "Forgive me, and you heal yourself. Tolerate me, and you invite more offense." Accepting people is not a righteous substitute for forgiving them. As a matter of fact, it is possible to forgive people of their sins without accepting their present actions. There is a world of difference between forgiveness and tolerance. You can forgive someone of anything, but you cannot tolerate everything.

The teachings of Jesus require us to forgive the offender seventy times seven for his past transgression, but they do not require us to remain in abusive situations.

Forgiveness is the act of believing the Word of God and making the conscious choice to release your offender from your desire for revenge. When we choose revenge over the way of forgiveness, we allow defilement into our essential identity.

7. *Perfectionism*

Perfectionism is the fear of failure expressed through an overcompensation to succeed at the expense of personal fulfillment. While many perfectionists often appear to be overachievers, their motivation is usually fueled by a desire to gain acceptance and to overcome a poor self-image.

On the surface, Rebecca seemed to be the perfect daughter. An only child, she was surrounded by the loving attention of her parents, and she returned the same back to them. She excelled in everything she took on in high school, from the debate team to the marching band. On more than one occasion she brought tears of joy to their eyes while standing on a platform to receive an award for her accomplishments. This talented young lady wanted to please her parents more than anything else in life.

From the time Rebecca was a child, her father joked, "This is our future doctor." When she graduated from high school as the salutatorian, there was no question about where she would be going next. Eight years later, she once again stood on the stage to receive a diploma, this time for top honors at medical school. Shortly after her graduation, she entered her residency at Hillcrest Medical Center. Everything in her life seemed to be perfect, except for one small thing—she was deeply unhappy and thoroughly unfulfilled.

In the midst of increasing depression, she scheduled a

few days of rest and relaxation. Perhaps some time away from the daily grind would recharge her batteries and energize her to resume the frenetic pace in which she lived. Early the second morning she experienced a devastating emotional breakdown. It came while she was eating breakfast. When faced with nothing to do that day, she did not know how to respond. *Just how long has it been since my life wasn't perfectly mapped out for me?* she wondered.

Frustrated with her lack of composure, she tried to pull herself together and couldn't. After three long days of soul-searching, with a trembling hand, she was finally able to reach for the telephone to call her father. The decision had been made; she was leaving her residency.

Like many others around us, Rebecca had become someone other than whom she was created to be. Her desire to please her parents had dominated her discovery of the divine design that The Image Maker had established for her life. She had settled for imitating life rather than living life.

How much of your life have you wasted in a futile attempt to gain the approval of others? In order to unveil your essential identity, you must give yourself the freedom to grow into who you are.

DISCOVERING THE DIVINE PERSPECTIVE

DESTINY ALWAYS BEGINS internally and eventually manifests itself externally. It comes from the inside out—not the outside in. That's why you can put a purposeful man in an oppressive environment, and given enough time, he will change it. But conversely, you can put a slothful man in an environment rife with potential, and he will never rise to greatness. Destiny is the result of understanding our essential identity, coming to terms with our security in the will of God and tapping into the passion for the journey.

Abraham changed the course of history because of an internal picture that was formed in his soul when he encountered The Image Maker on the backside of the desert. Moses brought deliverance to his generation because of an internal perspective that was formed when he encountered the great "I AM" in a burning bush. Joseph ruled a nation because of an internal perspective that was formed when he saw his potential in a dream. David served his generation because of an internal perspective of victory that was formed while tending his father's sheep.

Peter participated in the harvest of Pentecost because of an internal perspective that was formed when God's grace proved to be greater than his personal failures. Paul impacted the world like no other man because of an internal perspective that was formed when he was thrown from his donkey on the Damascus Road. So, as you can see, destiny always begins internally and eventually manifests itself externally. It begins with the development of an inner image of victory.

DEVELOPING THE INNER IMAGE

I AGREE WITH Harvard Business School professor Gary Hamel when he says, "Perspective is worth fifty IQ points."[4]

The real problem with most of us is that we have never worked long enough on establishing an inner image of victory deep in our soul (mind, will and emotions). We spend most of our time thinking about what we cannot accomplish in life, for whatever reason we believe that we cannot achieve it.

"Oh, I could never see myself doing that," we say. "I could never see myself having that." "Why, I'm just a woman in a man's world." Or we assert, "I'm just a black man in a white man's world. I don't have enough education; I'm lacking in qualified experience; I'll never reach my dreams; I'll never succeed!"

Rather than using the creative power of the redeemed spirit to chart a course of victory, many people use it to reinforce a lifestyle of defeat. Through spiritual ignorance, they curse the very thing God has chosen to prosper them in. And then they have the audacity to get angry with God! *Why isn't God blessing me?* they wonder. *Why does it seem that everyone else gets all the breaks? What do they have that I don't?* Maybe they don't have anything more than a tongue under divine control and an image of victory in their soul.

That's why Romans 12:2 says, "Do not be conformed to this world, but be transformed by the renewing of your mind, that you may prove what is that good and acceptable and perfect will of God."

Do you want to break free from your pointless existence? Do you really want to transform your life from hopelessness and despair to purpose and productivity? Then you must begin renewing your mind by the Word of God to the pathway He has chosen for your life. And as you do, The Image Maker will unveil your essential identity.

In order to break free from the bondage
of a defeated self-image, we must
reexamine the commonly accepted views of
the church and recover the apostolic
technology of the new creation.

Eight

THE TECHNOLOGY
OF THE NEW CREATION

IN THE NEW Testament epistles written by Paul the Apostle, we discover a spiritual technology concerning the identity of the new creation.

First a word about technology. The Oxford American Dictionary defines *technology* as "the scientific study of mechanical arts and applied sciences; these subjects, and their practical application in industry." For the sake of this chapter, I have chosen to define *technology* as "an action that produces a specific result when applied." Others have referred to this same principle as a "spiritual law" and have defined it as "a biblical principle that produces a specific result when set in motion."

In keeping with this paradigm, I have come to see Redemption as a spiritual technology—a spiritual action that produces a specific result when applied.

In his groundbreaking book, *Soul Tsunami*, Leonard Sweet expands the traditional view of technology:

> Unlike past technological innovations—agriculture, sailing ships, the printing press, gunpowder, industrialization, the automobile, atomic energy—it is now impossible to talk about anything without talking about technology. Technology is no longer a separate category. It does not exist on its own, but is intrinsic and implicit in life. Technology pervades everything and is a part of everything. Name an area or field of technology. Technology is now a part of everything—from sneakers to toothpaste, from genetics to religion, from you to me.... Technology is beyond even culture. It pervades who we are as people.[1]

The Old Testament narrative gives us veiled glimpses into The Image Maker's technology of Redemption. Through allegory, type and prophetic prose, we are pointed toward the ultimate event on which eternity hinges. By the time we reach Malachi, it is as if we were looking over the shoulder of the divine Architect as He turns the final page of the cosmic blueprint before lovingly crafting His masterpiece.

The New Testament centers around the unveiling of the express image, the technology of Incarnation made manifest in a corporal, material form. This is The Image Maker proving His love for humanity by sending the Prince of Heaven to reclaim, reconcile and restore man.

As we study the apostolic epistles, we are given insight

into the hidden mystery of the eternal purpose of Christ and His church. Through special revelation, these New Covenant apostles discovered the purpose of man, as he returns back to Eden and beyond, through the power of the new birth experience. With apostolic precision we are shown how the divine blueprint was systematically followed, line upon line, precept upon precept. The hidden mystery of the Old Covenant has now become "the mystery revealed." When describing the relationship of the Old Testament to the New, my hermeneutics instructor once said, "The New is in the Old *concealed;* the Old is in the New *revealed.*"

The technology of Redemption is not a "hit-or-miss" proposition. This spiritual force is not selectively distributed throughout the world, only finding application in the lives of an elite minority. It is a global operation—freely crossing national boundaries, racial barriers and class distinctions. Consistent with the nature of spiritual law, Redemption is a universally established principle, producing the same result in the life of every person who believes and receives. The work of Redemption will produce the same transformation in the life of any man who is willing to identify with the death, burial and resurrection of Jesus Christ.

We need to establish this great redemptive fact: God performed in Christ what He wanted to accomplish in every man—in every generation. God boldly asserted all that He had in Christ and then, by virtue of the Holy Spirit, supernaturally joined us to Him. If you do not know what the Father wanted to do in every man, simply look at Jesus Christ. Colossians 1:18 says, "He is the head of the body, the church, who is the beginning, the firstborn from the dead, that in all things He may have the preeminence." The word *beginning* means "the first person in a series, leader." The word denotes not merely the first in a series, but also the source to which the series can be traced. The word *firstborn* implies that because He is the first born, others will follow. The fact that He is the beginning indicates that their resurrection is due to His power. He is not only the first to rise, but of these risen ones He is the Master and Lord. Thus, He who is the Creator and Ruler of the Universe is likewise the Source and Sovereign of the new spiritual creation, the church.

A Limited View
Produces a Limited Atonement

In order to break free from the bondage of a defeated self-image, we must reexamine the commonly accepted views of the church and recover the apostolic technology of the new creation. A twenty-first-century view of these truths, however, affords us both advantages and disadvantages. We have the advantage of seeing the influence of the gospel and how it has changed the course of history. But we also have the disadvantage of viewing New Testament truth through the mosaic of religious interpretation. Like a man standing in the "house of mirrors" at a carnival, we find ourselves trying to determine which image is the real one.

Through this apostolic technology, the image of God in man, which was marred in the Fall, is being progressively revealed and restored. This implies that through this process, man's perverted view of self-image is being clarified and healed. This renewal of the self-image takes place in two specific areas.

First, when the Holy Spirit regenerates us, He also empowers us to resist arrogance and pride, the first perversions of the self-image. In place of those self-destructive elements, He leaves a deposit of thankfulness and humility. We often hear, "I'm just a sinner saved by grace." Although it may sound as if it comes from a posture of humility, those who subscribe to this quality of life lack foundational revelation. The whole purpose of being saved by grace is to remove you from your identity as a sinner. As tragic as it is, this mentality has kept many believers from living the ascended life, from living above the tempter and the habit patterns of the old self. This thinking erodes the apostolic image of all things being new in Christ.

The "once a sinner, always a sinner" view has been offset by the "I have a personal sovereignty" philosophy at the opposite end of the spectrum. One side is unable to comprehend the worthiness of man through God's abundant grace, while the other has moved into a pretense of human divinity that smacks of carnal arrogance. The truth of the matter can only be determined through New Testament revelation in stark contrast to certain aspects of Protestant Reformation that teach a weak doctrine of "limited atonement."

Many of these doctrines, in their most extreme applications, distort the issue of man's worthiness even to be saved. Others, though they may acknowledge Jesus Christ as the initiator of reconciliation, emphasize the work of man as the source of *securing* his own salvation through his good works, apart from grace.

The apostolic technology also speaks to the second type of perversion we have seen—namely an extremely low self-image. Unfortunately, many sincere Christians are more focused on their own personal weakness rather than on their newly developed image as the new creation. It takes an awareness of where you came from contrasted with the revelation of who you now are to maintain spiritual balance in your life.

THE APOSTOLIC CONCEPT OF
THE IMAGE OF GOD

A CAREFUL STUDY of Paul's writing reveals a "system of truth" that consistently defines his view of the image of God—lost by man, regained by Christ and restored in the new creation. This term, *system of truth*, was first coined by Richard Weymouth in his New Testament translation of Romans 6:17: "But thanks be unto God that you were once in thralldom to sin, but you have now yielded a hearty obedience to that *system of truth* in which you have been instructed" (emphasis added).

This system of truth reveals the technology of Redemption as it relates to the vicarious suffering, substitutionary death and glorious resurrection of Jesus Christ with the restoration of man as the central object of this action.

The death, burial and resurrection of Jesus Christ are the core of the gospel. The same power that God released in the *event* is in the *message*. The gospel perpetuates the same resurrection power that God released in Christ when He raised Him from the dead. Every other issue that has bearing on the abundant life flows from this "core value" that serves as the legal basis for our redemption, regeneration and continual deliverance.

> Knowing that you were not redeemed with corruptible things, like silver or gold, from your aimless conduct received by tradition from your fathers, but with the precious blood of Christ, as of a lamb without blemish and without spot.
>
> —1 PETER 1:18–19

The clearest definition of *redemption* is found in Webster's New World Dictionary and means "to buy back; to get back; to recover; to ransom; to pay off." It has often been said that the value of a thing is determined by the price one is willing to pay for it. The cost of our redemption is the highest price ever paid—for anything, for any reason. Our redemption was the greatest risk ever taken as divinity became subject to the frail human form. The greatest faith ever displayed was the faith of God in His Son. Before Redemption, the value of fallen man was undetermined.

It is important for us to see that the moral weakness of man did not take The Image Maker by surprise. The question is often asked: "If God is omniscient and omnipotent, why didn't He prevent the transgression of Adam in the Garden?" The answer is quite simple. The Image Maker designed Adam and Eve with the desire and ability to respond to His love, but He also created them with the freedom to accept or resist His sovereign authority. Knowing the deceptive nature of man's chief antagonist, the plan to redeem man was determined before he even sinned. Restoration begins in the mind of God before destruction ever takes place.

Only when we begin to understand the extent to which we have been redeemed will we release the faith necessary to walk in the fullness of Redemption. Our redemption is lacking absolutely nothing to complete it. "For as by one man's disobedience many were made sinners, so also by one Man's obedience many will be made righteous" (Rom. 5:19).

The Genesis account tells us what the curse consisted of:

- Man was driven from the presence of God and banned from eternal life.

- Enmity was released between the deceiver and all born of woman, leaving humanity engaged in spiritual warfare.

- The unity of the marriage covenant was placed under stress, giving way to relational disharmony.

- The parental connection was placed in jeopardy, allowing the entrance of pain in birthing and rearing children.

- The earth was cursed, resulting in drought, famine, pestilence, unstable weather patterns and geological upheaval.

- Man's toil was reduced to futility, striving to make a living. He left his position of abundance.

- Death entered into the world, both physically and spiritually.

The long-term effect of the curse, which came upon everything placed under Adam's dominion, was the gradual distortion of the divine imprint on man. Adam's sin was the beginning of sorrows, the source of all pain and evil, which the cosmos has experienced from that day until this. However, the prescription for breaking the curse was also included in its proclamation. In the great *protevangelium* of Scripture (*protevangelium* is a Latin word identifying Genesis 3:15 as the first declaration of the gospel[2]), the seed of the woman (Christ, the Son of Man) was destined to crush the head (the authority) of the serpent (the devil) according to Genesis 3:15.

Preparation for Redemption

In the midst of universal suffering, The Image Maker began to offer His blessing through contractual agreement. Through the Noahic Covenant, God's promise to preserve the earth was established. Through the Abrahamic Covenant, God's promise of a Redeemer from Abraham's lineage was established. Through the Mosaic Covenant, God's expectation for man was explained, the disobedience of man defined and the curse of the law revealed. Through the Davidic Covenant, God promises a King-Priest who will rule in the likeness of David. And then God established His final covenant with His Son, the Lord Jesus Christ. Through Christ, God renewed His covenant with the whole of creation.

Christ is the fulfillment of all the covenants previously made to Noah, Abraham, Moses and David. Through believing in and receiving His redeeming sacrifice, we are now included in His inheritance. The church, as the body of Christ, is continuing to participate in the proclamation and benefits of His covenant.

> He is the Mediator of the new covenant, by means of death, for the redemption of the transgressions under the first covenant, that those who are called may receive the promise of the eternal inheritance.
>
> —HEBREWS 9:15

In one supernatural moment, Redemption removes us out from under the curse and aligns us with the blessing of heaven. We no longer *are* who we once *were*. The apostolic technology reveals Redemption as a past tense experience. Just look at a few of the scriptures written by the apostle Paul.

> Christ has [past tense] redeemed us from the curse of the law.
>
> —GALATIANS 3:13

> The Father . . . has [past tense] qualified us to be partakers of the inheritance of the saints.
>
> —COLOSSIANS 1:12

> He [the Father] has [past tense] delivered us from the power of darkness and conveyed us into the kingdom of the Son of His love.
>
> —COLOSSIANS 1:13

Who [the Father] has [past tense] blessed us with every
spiritual blessing in the heavenly places in Christ.
—EPHESIANS 1:3

His divine power has [past tense] given to us all things
that pertain to life and godliness.
—2 PETER 1:3

WE WERE THERE

SITTING ON A pew, squirming between my mother and
brothers, I was confused by the words of the old Southern
spiritual song. Heads thrown back in joy, vocal chords
straining under the strength of their exuberance, the
choir sang:

> Were you there when they crucified my Lord?...
> Were you there when they laid Him in the tomb?...
> Were you there when He rose up from the dead?...[3]

To my six-year-old mind, the possibility seemed ludi-
crous. How could I have been *there* when I was just barely
here two thousand years later? Perhaps you have wondered
the very same thing.

Identifying with Christ means that as His spiritual seed
we realize we were *there*, even when we were not there.
Though absent in the flesh, we were in Christ in the form
of His elect—"chosen...in him before the foundation of
the world" (Eph. 1:4, KJV).

We were there when He suffered unjustly at the cruel
hands of His Roman oppressors.

We were there when He became the sacrifice that satisfied the justice of almighty God.

We were there when He experienced death in the flesh,
but victory over the powers of darkness.

We were there when He redeemed us by placing His

146

atoning blood on the mercy seat.

We were there when the Father raised Him from the grave, and He stood as our representative before the court of heaven.

We were there when He ascended, and we are forever seated with Him in heavenly places far above principalities and powers, not just as observers but as participants.

The Apostolic Image of the Church

Our true identity is what God's Word says about us. The apostolic technology provides us with a detailed description of our new identification. These are a few of our character qualities:

- We are called *members of Christ's body.* Each of us has an individual expression of the character and nature of the Son of God (Eph. 5:30).

- We are called *the sons of God.* This entitles us to share in all of Christ's character (1 John 3:1).

- We are called *Zion, the beloved city of God.* We are structured as a city of refuge in the midst of an environment hostile to our identity (Ps. 125:1).

- We are called *citizens of the heavenly Jerusalem.* We serve as ambassadors of the kingdom of God (Eph. 2:6; 6:20).

- We are identified as *one new man* symbolizing the unity we share with Christ (Eph. 2:15).

- We are the *bride of Christ,* chosen to be pure and undefiled (Rev. 21:2).

- We are *heirs and joint heirs with Christ.* As such, we share in Christ's inheritance (Rom. 8:17).

- We are called *soldiers in the army of the Lord*, with the right to exercise His authority in the world (2 Tim. 2:3–4).

The new creation is so unique and diverse that it cannot be identified by one single metaphor. It takes dozens of descriptive phrases throughout the whole of the Bible to even begin to identify who we are in Christ. Even then our individual identities are as diverse as our respective personalities. But as we discover our identity in Christ, His nature empowers us to reveal our unique expression.

BLINDED TO THE BLIND SPOT

IN ALMOST TWO decades of pastoral counseling, I've often encountered very sincere people who are being challenged by a friend or a spouse over an area of character that they themselves cannot see.

I remember one young man in particular who had a debilitating habit of verbally abusing his wife in order to bolster his distorted self-image. Devastated by years of humiliation, his wife finally convinced him to come for counseling since this problem was putting them in one embarrassing situation after another. When I approached the subject, the young man denied the problem, refusing to trust the insight of those closest to him. When I suggested that he might have a blind spot, he was appalled. There was no way that he, of all people, could have a blind spot. His exact words were, "I just can't see it; I am not that kind of person." Well, the funny thing about a blind spot is that you just can't see it.

We must come to trust the fact that The Image Maker is aware of those areas we successfully hide from others, along with those areas we have also hidden from ourselves. Before we can fully embrace the outworking of Redemption, we must acknowledge our need to be redeemed.

The Technology of the New Creation

BY IDENTIFYING WITH Adam, we qualify to identify with Christ. By identifying with Christ, we discover the truth about ourselves.

> For you died, and your life is hidden with Christ in God. When Christ who is our life appears, then you also will appear with Him in glory.
> —COLOSSIANS 3:3–4

Identifying with Christ as the Son of Man qualifies us to receive His sacrificial atonement for our fallen nature. Identifying with Christ as the Son of God qualifies us to receive the favored inheritance that the Father promised the Son and all who would believe on Him.

The apostle Paul phrases it this way:

> Therefore we were buried with Him through baptism into death, that just as Christ was raised from the dead by the glory of the Father, even so we also should walk in newness of life. For if we have been united together in the likeness of His death, certainly we also shall be in the likeness of His resurrection.
> —ROMANS 6:4–5

The technology of Redemption produces the same result in every man who is born of the Spirit of God. As a result of the vicarious suffering, substitutionary death and glorious resurrection of Jesus Christ, you are now redeemed, reconciled and restored. As the new creation, there is no trace left of the person you used to be in your inner man. All things have been made new through the power of His grace.

PART III:
DETERMINING YOUR
MISSION

Beginning with the entrance of original sin into the world, the spirit of condemnation began working to alienate man from the presence of The Image Maker. In every generation following, it has capitalized upon man's propensity toward sin consciousness, thereby blinding him to the opportunity to be accepted by God.

Nine

LIVING FREE FROM SIN CONSCIOUSNESS

As powerful and undeniable as the Scriptures make freedom from sin consciousness known, some still tend to think that the more conscious we are of sin, the less likely we are to commit acts of sin. But that perspective usually draws us toward increased sinfulness. Why? Because you will always move in the direction of your most dominant thought. That's why Proverbs 23:7 declares, "For as he thinks in his heart, so is he." Our meditation has the power to determine our destination.

Sin consciousness always results in increased sinfulness.

However, when we focus on righteousness, we leave little room for the works of iniquity to be found present in our lives. Righteousness is a spiritual force that if yielded to will cause our motivations, thoughts and intentions to be pure, just as Jesus is pure.

Our personal righteousness in Christ is a powerful weapon in the arsenal of the new creation, and yet so often we reduce its inherent power and authority, much like the timeworn phrase "born again." In today's consumer marketplace, we hear of "born-again" corporations, "born-again" sports teams and even "born-again" closets with just a little friendly assistance from any popular home improvement magazine. But righteousness is both a noun and a verb. It is who we are in conjunction with what we are empowered to do through the grace of God.

E. W. Kenyon once wrote, "The desire to get rid of sin consciousness has given birth to all of the major religions of the world. Few theologians have recognized the fact that sin consciousness is the parent of practically all human religions."[1]

What a powerful thought! Most people do not realize that religion is man's attempt to gain divine favor based upon *man's terms* rather than upon *God's terms*. At the root of all religion is man's search for significance. *Religion* is *man's acceptance* of God, but *Christianity* is *God's acceptance* of man. There is only one person in the universe who is qualified to accept you as you are—with implications for time and eternity. The last Adam (Jesus Christ) is the only one spiritually qualified to restore your broken relationship with The Image Maker. The first Adam sold the whole of humanity into spiritual slavery because of disobedience, but the last Adam redeemed mankind through His perfect obedience.

In an age when society defies the need for absolute truth, we discover that God has given us a flawless standard, seen only in the face of Jesus Christ. By *standard*, I mean a measuring rod of righteous perfection that defies the accusing voice of sin consciousness. The writer of Hebrews reveals how God carefully communicated His word of righteousness throughout the history of man, but has now and forever chosen to reveal its final expression through His Son, Christ Jesus. (See Hebrews 1:1–2.) When we see Jesus, we see the sum total of perfect righteousness, the same measure that is offered to all those who receive His provision.

What could be more gloriously intrusive than having your mind, will and emotions permanently invaded by the mind of Christ, as well as being empowered to walk free from the defiling presence of sin? If this were not attainable, then there would not be such overwhelming evidence in the Scriptures of not just the *foundations* of righteousness, but the glorious *effects* of righteousness as well. (See Isaiah 32:17.)

So few of us see ourselves as what Paul described in Romans 6:18—slaves of righteousness. As one enslaved to righteousness, we are given the opportunity to be shareholders in an incorruptible, undefiled quality of life—to have an unparalleled sense of equilibrium in our soul that enables us to walk through life with purpose and direction. This truly has to be the key to the quality of "abundant life" that Jesus described to His disciples.

Seeing but Not Perceiving

Beginning with the entrance of original sin into the world, the spirit of condemnation began working to alienate man from the presence of The Image Maker. In every generation following, it has capitalized upon man's propensity toward sin consciousness, thereby blinding him to the opportunity to be accepted by God. Living in a world of darkness, we accepted the lie that we were unworthy to enter the throne room, and we settled for our spiritual displacement. So, what is the solution for our self-imposed exile from the presence of God? We must train ourselves to perceive and believe what the Word of God has to say about our essential identity as the new creation. Until then, we can plainly point out specific passages that speak of freedom from guilt and shame, but our eyes are not quite fully open to what life could be like as a prisoner of hope and righteousness.

In his remarkable book *An Anthropologist on Mars*, Dr. Oliver Sacks tells the story of a man who had become blind as a child, yet regained his complete vision in midlife by way of a medical miracle. As the potential cure, along with its unpredictable outcome, was explained in detail, this man concluded that he would surely be no worse off even if the operation failed.

After a long, exacting surgery, Virgil's postoperative bandages were slowly removed, and for the first time in over forty years, he opened his eyes and could actually see. Dr. Sacks describes the first few moments following the removal of the bandages. "The moment of truth had finally come. Or had it? The dramatic moment stayed vacant, grew longer, sagged. No cry ('I can see!') burst from Virgil's lips. He seemed to be staring blankly, bewildered, without focusing, at the surgeon, who stood before him, still holding the bandages. Only when the surgeon spoke, saying, 'Well,' did a look of recognition cross Virgil's face."

When the light waves were finally able to penetrate past his prison of darkness, much to the dismay of his family, he found himself unprepared for this violent visual encounter. Dr. Sacks continues, "Virgil told me later that in his first moment he had no idea what he was seeing. There was light, there was movement, there was color, all mixed up, all meaningless, a blur. Then out of the blur came a voice that said, "Well?" Then, and only then, he said, did he finally realize that this chaos of light and shadow was a

156

face—and indeed, the face of the surgeon."

After further testing, it was discovered that Virgil could see images of people, light and color, and even his own reflection, but in the midst of all the visual stimuli, he remained "mentally blinded." In spite of his ability to see, he had no way of interpreting what all of the shapes, nuances and images meant—his cerebral capabilities had never been trained for a day like this.

Virgil's mind had suddenly been thrown into an environment common to all "sighted" people, but instead of accepting and interpreting what he saw, he found himself unsure, frightened and disoriented. To compound the frustration, his depth perception and reaction time were nonexistent. In order to comprehend his visual surroundings, Virgil's mind had to be trained to perceive his visual surroundings. He experienced what we Christians would call, in a spiritual sense, the renewing of his mind.

For forty dark years all of Virgil's previous experiences had come through a different sense—the sense of touch. As he handled the delicate, spongy petals of a rose, a signal would be sent to his brain creating a frame of reference for the image of a flower. But now that he could *see* a flower, it meant nothing to him unless aided by his sense of touch. The process was gradual, painful and at times halted, but Virgil finally began to connect with his "sighted" world. It was only when Virgil moved beyond *seeing* and moved into *perception* that he could begin to appreciate the beauty and significance of the world around him.[2]

This medical miracle is very similar to the story in the Gospel of Mark of the blind man who lived in Bethsaida. When Jesus touched his eyes *initially*, the blind man said he could "see men like trees, walking" (Mark 8:24). The next verse says, "Then He [Jesus] put His hands on his eyes *again* and made him look up. And he was restored and saw everyone clearly." It seems that the first touch restored this man's *vision*, but a second touch was needed to restore his *perception*.

This miracle targets our lives with precision. Like the blind man, our eyes were initially opened to see into the radiant world of three-dimensional color, and yet we only perceive limited shades of gray. Out of the slumber of sin consciousness, we were awakened to the infinite glory of our salvation, and yet we see men like trees, walking. We have a legitimate dilemma—we have sight, but no comprehension; we have vision, but no perception. We have seen the beauty of our salvation, but we must press on to break free from the mental blindness that holds us captive to a limited experience. We must earnestly seek to discover what it means to believe fully that "Christ is the end of the law" and the Burden-Bearer of the oppression of sin consciousness in our lives. (See Romans 10:4.) By growing in grace and the knowledge of the Lord Jesus Christ, we will develop the spiritual perception that is our birthright.

A. W. Tozer once said:

> They to whom the Word comes in power know this deliverance, this inward migration of the soul from slavery to freedom, this release from moral bondage. They know in experience a radical shift in position, a real crossing over, and they stand consciously on another soil under another sky and breathe another air. Their life motives are changed and their inward drives made new.[3]

It is high time for our generation to recover an understanding of what it means to live as the sons of God, free from shame and the destructive effects of sin consciousness.

Paul put it like this, "Awake to righteousness, and do not sin" (1 Cor. 15:34). The world is waiting for the awakening of those who have been made the righteousness of God in Christ. Creation is longing for the manifestation of those who have come to faith in whom The Image Maker created them to be through the miracle of the new birth experience.

> Through the Spirit, Christ offered himself as an unblemished sacrifice, freeing us from all those dead-end efforts to make ourselves respectable, so that we can live all out for God.
> —HEBREWS 9:14, THE MESSAGE

PRACTICE MAKES PERMANENT

WE HAVE HEARD it said, "Practice makes perfect." But that is not altogether true. In reality, practice makes permanent—whether right or wrong. As a tournament archer, I can assure you that the secret to hitting the bull's-eye consistently is not in strength or zeal—it is in correct form. In my early days of competition, I found myself practicing for weeks, only to discover on the day of the tournament that my form was wrong. Even though my bad form still allowed me to hit the target as I practiced in my backyard, under the pressure of the tournament I was unable to shoot with consistent accuracy. All of the long hours spent in practice only made my bad form permanent, not perfect. Correcting the problem was a matter of going back to the basics and reprogramming my mind to the information needed to adjust my form.

I believe the primary reason most Christians struggle with an overwhelming degree of sin consciousness is because they have not had a revelation of what it means to live righteous consciously. Therefore, we find ourselves consistently defeated in the battlefield of life, struggling just to maintain a mere semblance of Christian living. This lack of revelation leaves us insecure in the presence of God, wondering whether or not we are really accepted in the Beloved. The work of Redemption is unquestioned in the heavens among principalities and powers, and yet ironically, it is still doubted among the sons of men. What we have practiced has now become permanent.

Practicing condemnation, either on ourselves or on those around us, gives a permanent foothold to this spiritually debilitating force. Left untreated, the force of condemnation eventually breaks down the spiritual immune system, destroying our confidence in God and breeding insecurity in our identity as His sons. Condemnation aborts spiritual confidence. Condemnation destroys spiritual security.

> For if our heart condemns us, God is greater than our heart, and knows all things. Beloved, if our heart does not condemn us, we have confidence toward God.
> —1 JOHN 3:20–21

Did you perceive that? God is greater than your self-imposed condemnation! His grace is infinitely greater than your personal weakness.

At the root of all condemnation is a lie that says, "You're not worthy enough…God doesn't really accept you…You will never become who you should be." When condemnation is allowed to operate, it eventually drowns out the voice of confidence. And without confidence, we cannot possibly please God. Confidence is the core of faith. Condemnation reduces us to crawling tentatively into the presence of God as intruders rather than entering boldly as sons in whom the Father is well pleased!

IMITATION OR EMANATION

ONE OF THE most forceful chapters in the New Testament relating to being liberated from sin consciousness is Hebrews 10.

> For the law, having a *shadow* of the good things to come, and not the *very image* of the things, can never with these same sacrifices, which they offer continually year by year, make those who approach perfect. For then would they not have ceased to be offered? For the worshipers, once purified, would have no more *consciousness of sins*. But in those sacrifices there is a *reminder* of sins every year.
>
> —HEBREWS 10:1–3, EMPHASIS ADDED

This writer by revelation goes on to clearly define the difference between shadow and substance. In verse 10, he announces, "By that [His] will we have been sanctified through the offering of the body of Jesus Christ once for all." Verse 14 states, "For by one offering He has perfected forever those who are being sanctified." Verse 22 reads, "Let us draw near with a true heart in full assurance of faith, having our hearts sprinkled from an evil conscience and our bodies washed with pure water."

The New American Standard renders a part of Hebrews 10:1 this way: "…not the very *form* of things…" (emphasis added). There are several definitions in the Greek language for the word *form*. In this passage it is the word *eikon*. It means an exact replica, representation or "picture" of an original. This word always assumes a prototype, which it not only resembles, but from which also it is *drawn*. This is the difference between "imitation and emanation." To *imitate* means to copy, mimic and follow an outward pattern, whereas *emanation* means to proceed or spring up out of an original source.

Hebrews 1:3 says that Jesus is the radiance of His glory and the exact representation of His nature. The Centenary Translation says, "He being an *emanation* of God's glory and stamp of His substance upholds the universe by the utterances of His power." Keep the word *form* in your thinking as we progress.

> …once *purified*, would have had no more consciousness of sins.
> —HEBREWS 10:2, EMPHASIS ADDED

> By that will we have been *sanctified*…
> —HEBREWS 10:10, EMPHASIS ADDED

> …having our hearts *sprinkled*…our bodies *washed*…
> —HEBREWS 10:22, EMPHASIS ADDED

Each one of these words—*purified, sanctified, sprinkled* and *washed*—are in what the Greek language calls the perfect tense. This tense conveys a "completed action that has lingering effects or that leaves an ongoing result or condition." Well-known grammarians H. W. Smyth and E. Burton describe an event in the perfect tense as a "completed action, the effects of which still continue in the present" and a past action that "affirms an existing result." Very often, the phrase *"and now still is"* aptly recaptures the meaning of the perfect tenses in Scripture.[4] My ambition is not so much to intrigue you with the Greek language, as it is to impact you with the language of Redemption!

Now, before you faint under the weight of this linguistic overload, let's look at some other passages that will clarify the "now still is" aspect of these "perfect tenses."

> He has *inherited* [and now still has] a more excellent name than they.
> —HEBREWS 1:4, NAS, EMPHASIS ADDED

> Jesus, because of the suffering of death *crowned* [and now still is] with glory and honor.
> —HEBREWS 2:9, NAS, EMPHASIS ADDED

> Jesus…who for the joy set before Him endured the
> cross…and *has sat down* [and now still is seated] at the
> right hand of the throne of God.
> —HEBREWS 12:2, NAS, EMPHASIS ADDED

Perhaps most often conveyed by the perfect tense, however, is the continuance of the *effect* of the action (not the
action itself). For example, the cry of Jesus from the cross,
"It is finished!" (John 19:30), is in the perfect tense, showing
us that the *results* and *effects* of His sacrificial death are anything but over and finished. The phrase "It is finished"
trumpets the end of the old order and the sacrifice that the
priests offered yearly in an attempt to make perfect those
who drew near to God. The old order is over; sin consciousness has been mastered by righteousness once and for all; yet
the *effects* of that freedom are anything but over. In this particular passage from John we get a clearer understanding
about the passages we have looked at previously in Hebrews.

In light of this explanation, let me summarize and
personalize these passages from Hebrews 10. "And having
once been cleansed, sanctified, sprinkled and washed in a
historical moment in time by the completed action of
Christ's redemptive work, I now have a lingering, ongoing
effect that still continues in my present. His past action of
death, burial, resurrection and ascension affirms an existing
up front, close and personal result in my life."

We have to realize that Redemption is an eternal event. We
acknowledge the proper time and place in history, because
the events surrounding the death, burial and resurrection
constitute history. But they are more than just biographical
facts—they are eternal events. This is why Jesus was the
"…Lamb slain from the foundation of the world" (Rev. 13:8).

When we accepted Christ, we accepted *freedom* from sin
consciousness—a freedom that continues to have a present

163

application in my life and yours. This freedom is greater than my personal ability to keep the law—it is a power that will not surrender under the crushing shame of personal failure.

SUBSTANCE OR SHADOW

NOW LET'S TAKE another look at the promise of deliverance from sin consciousness. As we saw earlier, Hebrews 10:1 describes the Law as a shadow that could never, by sacrifices, make perfect those who drew near; therefore, they remained with a sin consciousness. However, what Christ accomplished as the *form* (substance) was absolute and unconditional deliverance for all who believe and receive. Because of Jesus, we do not have to labor under the heavy, oppressive taskmaster of sin consciousness.

Now watch this principle: If I choose the Law, which was but a shadow, I will remain with a constant reminder of my sin and never break free from a consciousness of it. However, if I choose the substance—Christ and His forever settled work of righteousness—I will come out of the poverty of sin consciousness and move into the wealth of a "rightness with God" mind-set! (Christ has imparted to us His form—His very substance. And contained in that substance is His very mind, His personal thoughts). We are not living under the overwhelming weight of the Law any longer. We have moved out from under the shadow, which resulted in a constant reminder of sin, into the substance of Light, where we live in a constant reminder of righteousness.

As Eugene Peterson so powerfully puts it in Romans 6:3 of *The Message Bible:* "We left the old country of sin behind...we entered into the new country of grace—a new life in a new land!" A whole new world has opened up to us, which results in a constant reminder of righteousness. It is foreign to the spiritual nature of the new creation to be a slave to sin consciousness!

Living Free From Sin Consciousness

In John 8:36 we read, "If the Son liberates you...you are really and unquestionably free" (AMP). By the power of the Holy Spirit, your new identify is marked, and your position is sure. Insight has become your birthright, and you have awakened to "rightness with God" rather than living as a lonely exile in the land of sin consciousness.

SYNTHETIC OR ORGANIC RIGHTEOUSNESS

THE PROPER PLACE to regain our sight is to return back to where we lost it. Since we've already examined the Fall of man and his subsequent separation from God, let's take a look at The Image Maker's covenant with Abraham, which continued on with Christ and is now made available to you.

In Genesis 15, we discover the second mention (the first being Adam) of God opening a man's heart and eyes to a revelation of the divine intention for mankind. As a result of what Abraham saw, his entire world shifted into an awareness of his right standing with God.

Even though there was no established law to be accountable to during this time, God introduced the possibility of righteousness on the basis of believing. Rather than manufacturing righteousness through striving to perform good deeds, Abraham was considered righteous because of his trust in the almighty God. The simplicity of this act must capture our hearts lest we be driven into a state of synthetic or artificial righteousness. By *synthetic*, I mean something that is not derived from an organic source. Synthetic righteousness is produced by something other than faith in, and continuing relationship with, the Son of God.

Romans 10:5 reminds us, "For Moses writes about the righteousness which is of the law, 'The man who does those things shall live by them.'" Many Christians seem subconsciously to have adopted the position that we are *saved* by grace, yet *kept* by works. If your acceptance *with* God is based on synthetic righteousness (your own good deeds), then you can only be *kept* on the same basis. Self-earned righteousness is the breeding ground for spiritual insecurity—it always leaves you wondering, *If I earned this spiritual inheritance, will I be disinherited when I fail?*

The vicious cycle of synthetic righteousness plays out this way. When you miss the mark, you are spiritually susceptible to the torment of guilt and condemnation, which gives place to sin consciousness. Finally coming to your senses, you break free from the snare of sin, repent for your actions and then almost imperceptibly begin to feel that you need to "pay for your sins." After attempting to work your way back into God's good graces (which is a lesson in futility), you settle for a sense of spiritual insecurity.

Jesus Christ is the end of all synthetic efforts to be right with the Father, and through sharing in the righteousness that He obtained on our behalf, we are brought into a supernatural righteousness. The trail to and from Mount Sinai is well worn, with previous generations blindly following the same trail of despair. We were desperately in need of a forerunner, a pioneer, if you will, to blaze a new path for us to a new mountain, to receive a new covenant. Robing Himself in the frailty of humanity, living, suffering and dying as a man, the only begotten Image Bearer paved a ten-lane highway into the favor of God for all those who put their trust in Him. As the new creation, we now stand under the open skies of divine favor from our new vantage point on Mount Zion where we take our joy in the New Covenant of His grace.

THE RESULTS OF SIN CONSCIOUSNESS

As I MENTIONED in a previous chapter, I believe that the church has majored on behavior modification instead of focusing on identity revelation. The real problem with behavior modification is that it may leave you with a change of conduct, but it is powerless to impart righteousness, peace and joy. Following the warning to "taste not, touch not and handle not," we are preserved (for the moment) from failing, but we are left without any sense of purpose in life. Circling the wagons around the camp may protect you for a siege or two, but it will take you nowhere on the journey toward your inheritance in Christ. There is a better way to walk free from the power of sin.

When you begin to live in the reality of who you were made to be in Christ Jesus, then even hell itself cannot stop you. When you fully awaken to righteousness, temptation cannot destroy you, personal failure cannot abort your purpose and condemnation can no longer hold you captive. Your identity as a son of the Highest authorizes you to live in this world, even as He lived in this world. You are a king-priest, anointed to rule over the powers of darkness and to minister life to those around you. Open your eyes to the wonder of who you are! As you live and move and have your being in Christ, you are forever secure in your position as a son of righteousness.

Seeing the Problem, Prescribing the Cure

Before we conclude this study on living free from sin consciousness, I want to take a brief look at the poisonous effects of sin consciousness, along with the spiritual antidote.

The effects of sin consciousness are as follows:

- Condemnation
- Guilt
- Unworthiness
- Insecurity
- Weak faith
- Depression
- Shame
- Torment
- Self-rejection

- Struggling to feel accepted by God and others
- Lacking the freedom and boldness to enter the Father's presence

The solution to sin consciousness is found in renewing your mind with the following principles from the Word of God:

- I have been created in the image of God (Gen. 1:26).
- I have been regenerated into the likeness of God (John 3:6).
- I have confidence that God loves and accepts me (Eph. 1:6).
- As a son of God, I am pure from the defilement of the world (1 John 3:3).
- When I fail, God will not abandon me (Heb. 13:5).
- As I walk in the Spirit, I am free from condemnation (Rom. 8:1).
- As I love God and others, I increase my capacity to feel loved (1 John 4:12).
- As I love God and others, I am free from fear (1 John 4:18).
- As His child, I am always welcome in the presence of God (Heb. 10:19).
- My personal worth is based upon the price Jesus paid for my Redemption, not upon my personal ability to perform correctly every time I am confronted with temptation.
- God has a plan for my life that involves the fulfillment of my personal destiny.

- Even though I have faults and failures, I want to change. God is working to change me one step at a time. Furthermore, while I am in the process of changing, I can still enjoy life.

- Because I am accepted of God, I can accept others. As I sow seeds of unconditional acceptance, I will reap a harvest of unconditional acceptance.

Every righteous father desires to reproduce himself in his sons. This is what The Image Maker accomplished in us through the ongoing incarnation.

Ten

INVITING THE INCARNATION

T HE INCARNATION SERVES as the ultimate model of reconciliation. If the most basic need of fallen man was psychological, The Image Maker would have sent us a psychologist. If our emptiness could have been filled by the Law, He would have sent us a lawyer. But He wanted to teach us about personhood, so He sent us a person—the Word made flesh—not only to show us what the divine image is like, but also to show us how life is to be lived.

The prophet Isaiah revealed the divine intention concerning the Incarnation of the Hope of Israel:

Therefore the Lord Himself will give you a sign:
Behold, the virgin shall conceive and bear a Son, and
shall call His name Immanuel.

—ISAIAH 7:14

When this silver-tongued prophet poetically declared that
the "Lord Himself" would provide the sign, he used the
Hebrew title *Adonai*. This descriptive title literally means
"the Ruling One," who shall on His own terms, in His own
manner and at His own time perform this miraculous sign.

The coming Messiah was predestined to be called
Immanuel, which means "God with us" or, more literally
translated, "Incarnation." Jesus was conceived through the
supernatural intervention of the Holy Spirit overshadowing
the virgin womb of a young Israeli who had never known a
man and was to be acknowledged forever as the Incarnate
One. This Child was destined to be called "Incarnation."

The word *incarnate* simply means, "to embody in flesh, to
put into or represent in concrete, tangible form." The
Incarnation was the means through which The Image Maker
bridged the chasm between sinless Deity and sinful
humanity. Following the Fall of man, the human condition
steadily worsened until it settled in man's lowest estate.
Hearing the cry of lonely men to be accepted back into the
family of God, The Image Maker devised a means by which
one could legally reenter His presence without fear or shame.
The Incarnation was the Creator's answer to the universal cry
of man to be accepted.

THE BRIDGE BETWEEN TWO WORLDS

THE BRILLIANT CHAMPION of orthodoxy, Athanasisus, once
said:

What was God to do in the face of the dehumanizing
of humankind, this universal hiding of the knowledge

of Himself by the wiles of evil spirits? What else could He possibly do but renew His image in humankind, so that through it people might once more come to know Him? And how could this be done save by the coming of the very image Himself, our Savior Jesus Christ? Human beings could not have done it, for they are only made after the image: nor could have angels done it, for they are not the images of God. The Word of God came in His own person, because it was He alone, the image of the Father, who could recreate human beings made after the image.[1]

The Incarnation of sinless deity into the womb of a woman produced One who stood as man's mediator, being equal with God and yet united with man. He bridged the gap between a Holy God and an unholy race, bringing the two together on God's terms. As One who was fully God and yet fully man, He was uniquely qualified to assume the sins of the world, satisfy the judgment of the Father and fulfill the divine intention to provide a spiritual and legal basis for the destruction of man's archenemy.

Jesus Christ was no less than the mediator between two worlds. As heaven's representative on the earth, He revealed the Father "full of grace and truth." As earth's representative in the heavenlies, He revealed the Father's love for fallen man before all creation. At one and the same time, as a man, He lived a human life; as the Word, He was the sustaining life of the universe; and as a Son, He was in constant union with the Father.

NEW BEGINNINGS FOR MANKIND

THE FIRST CHAPTER of the Gospel of John serves as the New Testament counterpart of the Book of Genesis. It is a spiritual overlay of the Old Testament book of beginnings, therein revealing the pattern for kingdom living. John begins his opening statement by establishing the basis for the Incarnation.

Now remember what we saw in chapter one: Beginnings determine endings. This is God's first opportunity to project Himself into this time and space world, and He does so with careful consideration and deliberate intention. First impressions are lasting.

> In the beginning was the Word, and the Word was with God, and the Word was God.... And the Word became flesh and dwelt among us.
>
> —JOHN 1:1, 14

He was not just a babe lying in a manger. He was fundamentally different from every other child born in Bethlehem on that cool fall evening. This infant wrapped in swaddling clothes and lying innocently in the carefully arranged straw contained the spiritual blueprint for the restoration of man and the destruction of man's enemy. In spite of His unassuming posture, this helpless child of Mary was the only hope for hurting humanity.

> Veiled in flesh the Godhead see;
> Hail th'incarnate Deity.

In an age when mankind is desperately peering into the mystical dimension, hoping to catch a glimpse of deity, we need to be reminded of this one simple truth—if you want to see God, look at the baby in the manger. In one moment of decision, after nine months of gestation, God has become one of us so we might become one with Him. C. S. Lewis once said, "The Son of God became man to enable men to become the sons of God."

When commenting on this event, J. I. Packer wrote:

Incarnation gave the eternal Son of God capacity for this experience. "The Word became flesh" in the sense that without ceasing to be anything that He was before, He added to Himself all that humanness in this world involves—namely, life through a body bounded by space and time, with all the glories, limitations, and vulnerabilities that belong to our everyday existence, including in due course leaving behind the body through which one has consciously lived all along. Shakespeare, we know, acted in the plays he authored and produced, and that is a faint parallel to the co-Creator living an ordered creaturely life within His own created world.[2]

HYPOSTATIC UNION

THEOLOGIANS DESCRIBE THIS state of being as the "hypostatic union," which is just as much a mystery to most people as the principle itself. Quite frankly, I find it difficult to understand fully how Jesus could be totally God and completely man at the same time. It's far easier for me to comprehend His sinless life, earthly ministry, substitutionary death and glorious resurrection than to understand the mystery of the Incarnation itself.

Athanasisus continued on with these words:

> The solidarity of humankind is such that, by virtue of the Word's indwelling in a single body, the corruption that goes with death has lost all its power over all. You know how it is when some great king enters a large city and dwells in one of its houses. Because of his dwelling in that single house, the whole city is honored, and enemies and robbers cease to molest it. Even so is it with the King of all; He has come into our country and dwelt in one body amidst the many, and in consequence,

the designs of the enemy against humankind have been foiled, and the corruption of death, which formerly held them in its power, has simply ceased to be.[3]

THE IMPRINT OF THE FATHER

THE FINAL WORDS God spoke before leaving Israel in four hundred years of deafening silence were these:

> Behold, I will send you Elijah the prophet before the coming of the great and dreadful day of the LORD. And he will turn the hearts of the fathers to the children, and the hearts of the children to their fathers, lest I come and strike the earth with a curse.
>
> —MALACHI 4:5–6

When John the Baptist broke the silence of heaven ten generations later, he did so in the spirit and power of Elijah, restoring the connection between the heavenly Father and His wayward sons. In both the spiritual and natural realms, John began the process of "generational unification." His ministry prepared the way for man to be reconciled to God and to one another. Two thousand years later we are still trying to get it right.

The Image Maker's purpose in uniting fathers and sons was in order for the progeny to regain their identity so that they might fulfill their divine destiny. In a sociological, psychological and spiritual sense, it is the imprint of the Father that instills a sense of true identity in the child.

Perhaps you are one who struggles with a lack of worth and value because you were raised in a home with an absentee father. If that is the case, then may this be a word of deliverance for you. You have a Father. You have a heavenly Father who lovingly crafted you, who continually cares for you and will not leave you nor forsake you. Even when you did not merit His love, He cared enough to send His only begotten Son to rescue you from the powers of darkness that were destroying you. You have a loving "Dad" who is more committed to your spiritual development and ultimate purpose than you are.

Every righteous father desires to reproduce himself in his son. I distinctly remember daydreaming as a young father as I anticipated the spiritual, physical and emotional development of my three sons.

On a hot summer night, I stood in the delivery room of Kansas City hospital watching in stunned silence as my wife gave birth to my firstborn. Nothing had prepared me for the human drama unfolding before my eyes. While the child-birthing classes we attended in preparation were mildly informative, I actually experienced very little emotion and even less adrenaline while attending them. But what I witnessed in the delivery room that night drained the blood from my brain and left me with a dry mouth and sweaty palms. Seeing my condition, a wise nurse pulled a hospital gurney up next to my wife and ordered me to lie down beside her!

After recuperating from the shock of seeing the birth process, I was then confronted with another unexpected situation. I found myself completely unprepared for this tiny infant's absolute dependency and utter inadequacy. Thank God, my wife was far more mature than I was, and the baby was well cared for.

For all practical purposes, this tiny infant had no real capacity to contribute to the family mission. Weak, whiny, constantly hungry and unexpectedly stinky, this baby was totally dependent upon his mother and me to care for him without regard to our own personal needs. Many times while changing a diaper or burping him in the middle of the night, I thought, *I can't wait until he grows up and begins to contribute something meaningful around here.* I longed for the day when he could hunt, fish and climb mountains with me. And I couldn't wait to start all over again with the second child. By then, I considered myself an expert.

As our three sons progressed through early childhood development, demonstrating the cognizant skills of speech, movement and reason, I saw myself in almost every action they took. Some of those actions were cause for joy; others were cause for personal adjustment and parental correction. For good and bad, I had successfully reproduced myself in my sons.

Someone once said, "Christianity is Christ received, realized and reproduced." The very genius of Christianity is the Father's ability to reproduce Himself in our lives through the implement of His life-producing Word. Through the new birth experience, the Father once again takes humanity into partnership with Himself, allowing us to give birth to His eternal purpose. The Image Maker is in the process of developing the family business of "Jesus Christ and Sons."

THE ONGOING INCARNATION

As SHOCKING AS it may seem to one who has never heard this principle before, the Incarnation did not end with the birth of the only begotten Son of God. The New Testament writers eventually lead us beyond the Incarnation of Christ into the ongoing incarnation of the present-day body of Christ. Just as the Word became flesh in Jesus Christ, the new creation has been born again, "not of corruptible seed but incorruptible, through the word of God which lives and abides forever" (1 Pet. 1:23). This ongoing incarnation does not transform man from humanity to deity, but it does unite his spirit with the Lord in eternal union.

You see, the first-century church had discovered this to be true. And it became so real to them that their actions

178

resulted in their first being called "Christians" at Antioch. The term *Christian* literally means "little Christs" or "little anointed ones." This term was probably not a complimentary one to begin with. I suspect it was a derogatory term leveled by their detractors, and yet it reveals that even the world recognized that these first-century believers were living their lives in the image and likeness of the Son of God.

This is the process of the ongoing Incarnation. Just as the Word became flesh in Bethlehem, the Word continues to become flesh in Antioch. This is the next generation of believers, one step removed from personal and physical contact with Jesus Christ, also embodying the gospel. Even though the theological community has attempted to water down this principle by calling it the "incarnational presence," this is more literally rendered the "Incarnational Word." The Word of God, unrestrained, contains the power to reproduce itself over and over and over again.

FULFILLING THE ULTIMATE GOAL

LET ME ASK you an important question. What is the mission of the church? The answer is to be the body of which Christ is the Head. We have been divinely crafted to be the completion of Christ in the same way that a head needs a body in order to complete a person. The church is called to complete the Person of Christ. Now at first glance that statement may sound like heresy. You may be wondering, *Now, wait a minute. How can Jesus Christ be incomplete?* He cannot be incomplete in His essence or His character. He always has been and always will be God. But He is incomplete in His ultimate mission. Just as you need your body in order to complete your assignment on earth, so does Jesus Christ!

The analogy of the human body is Paul's favorite description of the church, so let's take another look at this picture. What is the job of your body? It has one primary purpose, and that is to fulfill the dictates of your head. When your brain says, "Move your arm," you move your arm. When your brain says, "Walk over to the refrigerator and pour yourself a glass of milk," you do exactly that.

If your brain says one thing and your body does another, you have disorder, and you cannot fulfill your purpose. Your body is the reflection of your brain. If you are undisciplined in your thinking, it will physically show in your body, in the way you carry yourself, how you walk, talk and dress. When you begin to train your brain by renewing your mind to the Word of God, then it will show in your physical man as well. Your body is designed to obey your head. And in a like sense, we are the body that has been lovingly designed and carefully crafted to obey the Head, the Lord Jesus Christ.

With nearly fifty years of history in classical Pentecostalism, Pastor Tommy Reid wrote:

> I believe the greatest revelation of the Holy Spirit to the church today is who we are in Christ. Until we learn that we are the ongoing incarnation, and until we learn our union with Him, and His union with us, we cannot comprehend the truth of Christianity.[4]

Union with Christ is the central theme of the plan of regeneration and the subsequent overcoming life. According to the words of Paul, the church is now one with Christ in His crucifixion (Gal. 2:20). We are one with Him in His resurrection (Gal. 2:20). We are one with Him in His glorious ascension (Eph. 2:6). We are one with Christ in His overcoming life. We are one with Him in His ongoing mission to restore that which was lost by Adam in the Garden of Eden. This is the spiritual reality of the Incarnation.

I love what F. J. Huegel once wrote in his classic book *Bone of His Bone*: "The Christian life is a participation, not an imitation."[5] The commands given us in the Bible are impossible to an imitator but not to a participant.

God is in the process of performing the very same thing in your life as He did in the life of Jesus Christ. Because of your trust in His Son, you have become a necessary agent in the ongoing work of reconciling all things back to the Father. The New Covenant order of reconciliation is, "God...in Christ reconciling the world to Himself" (2 Cor. 5:19). And in keeping with the principles of progressive revelation, He has committed unto the new creation this work of reconciliation. Through incarnational living, we are empowered to represent Him appropriately to the world.

This is why the apostles could use such revolutionary language when describing the nature of the new creation: "Ye are the body of Christ, and members in particular" (1 Cor. 12:27, KJV). What a powerful concept! To be joined with the God of glory through the investment of His Word in our lives is not an easy concept to grasp. I am convinced that we simply have accepted that descriptive term as just another religious slogan, like "Cleanliness is next to godliness." I'm sure you know what I mean. This is a phrase that communicates a moral truth, but really isn't as true as other more important truths are true.

THIS IS A GREAT MYSTERY

THERE ARE MYSTERIES beyond our grasp that are bound up inexplicably in the supernatural selection of Mary, the overshadowing of the Holy Spirit and the miraculous conception of Jesus. How can one be fully God and yet fully man? It is incomprehensible how the Son of God operated within the boundaries of human limitation so as to contain His Deity on the pathway to the cross. But this is fact—Bible

181

fact to be more specific—not twenty-first-century fiction.

When addressing the Ephesians church concerning the wonder of the Incarnation, Paul said:

> And He put all things under His feet, and gave Him to be head over all things to the church, which is His body, the fullness of Him who fills all in all.
> —EPHESIANS 1:22–23

The apostle related this spiritual reality to the marriage union in Ephesians 5. As the husband is head of the wife, he writes in verse 23, so also is Christ the head of the church. He continues on to say, "He who loves his wife loves himself. For no one ever hated his own flesh, but nourishes and cherishes it, just as the Lord does the church. *For we are members of His body*" (Eph. 5:28–30, emphasis added).

"This is a great mystery," Paul concludes, "but I speak concerning Christ and the church" (v. 32).

I know it's difficult to grasp. I realize that it's impossible to wrap your mind around this one; that's why Paul calls it a *great* mystery. The great mystery is this: How can we be joined as the members of the body of a man who lived two thousand years ago, was crucified for the sins of the world, was buried for three days and then rose again, only to ascend into heaven and become seated on the right hand of the Father? And furthermore, how can we, as mere mortals, be joined to one who is the sovereign God? Not only is this mystery "great" in the sense of being magnanimous, earth shaking and world changing, it is also "great" in the sense of being extraordinary.

The word *mystery* is the Greek word *musterion*, which simply means "a secret that can only be known to the initiated." You see, this incarnational principle can only be understood by those who have genuinely experienced it and have come to accept it as God's model for reconciliation in the earth. Even then, this mystery is still far too radical, frightening and mystical for many Christians to grasp.

Many Christians still see themselves as the same old fallen man with a new set of friends and somewhere exciting to go on Sunday morning. To consider that God Himself became flesh and bone before calling us to share in His joy by carrying on the family business is more than some can accept. It is much easier to think of God as a distant relative who only shows up on on Easter and Christmas just to keep the family tradition alive.

I believe there were many in the first-century church who had the same difficulty in processing this truth, as do many Christians today. That's why Paul repeated himself on more than one occasion saying, "For we are members of His body, of His flesh and of His bones" (Eph. 5:30).

BECOMING ONE WITH CHRIST

PAUL REVEALS THE incarnation principle with such descriptive force that he warns us against immorality on the basis of joining Christ's body to the body of a harlot.

> Do you not see and know that your bodies are members (bodily parts) of Christ (the Messiah)? Am I therefore to take the parts of Christ and make [them] parts of a prostitute? Never! Never! Or do you not know and realize that when a man joins himself to a prostitute, he becomes one body with her? The two, it is written, shall become one flesh. [Gen. 2:24.] But the person who is united to the Lord becomes one spirit with Him.
> —1 CORINTHIANS 6:15–17, AMP

When you are born again, your spirit is joined (fused together) with the Lord Jesus Christ, and you become one spirit with Him. Weymouth's translation says, "But he that is in union with the Master is one with Him in spirit." The

Living Bible says, "But if you give yourself to the Lord, you and Christ are joined together as one person."

As radical as this may seem, this is not figurative speech. This is not symbolic imagery. This eternal truth is mysteriously supernatural. The church is the "mystical body of Christ." Don't water this principle down! Don't rationalize it away! Read it, believe it and receive it!

This is what the ongoing incarnation means. Concerning the Incarnation, Frederick Buechner once said, "It is untheological. It is unsophisticated. It is undignified. But according to Christianity, it is the way things are."[6] The thought of being incarnated as the Word of God is almost too awesome a thought to fully comprehend, and yet in spite of our difficulty in understanding this great mystery, the gift goes on.

Hebrews 2:10 declares, "For it was fitting for Him, for whom are all things and by whom are all things, in bringing many sons to glory..." *Many* sons, not simply one Son. Jesus Christ is the head of this many-membered body often described as the "church." The divine order of the Incarnation is God in Christ, followed by Christ in you, the hope of glory.

INCARNATIONAL LIVING

LET'S LOOK AT seven vital principles of incarnational living.

1. You are not the same person that you once were.

Even though your actions may still be the same, remember that *you* are not the same. Living in Christ has absolutely nothing at all to do with your human *feelings*. It has everything to do with the completed sacrifice of God's own Son and the integrity of His eternal Word. Your current struggles do not evidence who you are at the core of your being. After the new birth experience, you are the "new man" striving to overcome rather than the "old man" struggling to reform. The basis of your essential identity has changed, and you are a new creature in Christ.

2. *Your future is not the same as it once was.*

Along with a transformation of identification, you also experienced a radical alteration of your destination. The new birth not only redeems your identity, but it also restructures the patterns of life that result in your destiny. Your future has now been reconciled with the plans and purposes that God has for your life.

3. *Even though you are the new creation, you still need the anointing to succeed in life.*

Your new identity is not enough to get you through the distressing challenges that every individual encounters at some point in their walk with God. Although Jesus was fully God, as a man He had to rely upon the power of the anointing in order to succeed. (See Acts 10:38.) The *anointing* is the empowering agent that energizes the new creation with the life of heaven. Through the power of the Holy Spirit, we continually experience increasing dimensions of the glory of God in our lives.

4. *Your potential in life is unlimited.*

The purpose of the cross was to defeat the power of the enemy and to reconcile men back to God, thereby removing every fleshly limitation from your life. All things are possible to the new creation that receives the Word of God as the pattern for living. As Paul boldly confessed, so must we: "I can do all things through Christ who strengthens me" (Phil. 4:13).

5. *You must guard your new life in Christ.*

Once you understand who you are and whom you represent, you will become careful with your actions in life.

Even those actions that may be "acceptable" for others may not be conducive to your life's purpose. The word *saved* means to be "daily delivered from sin's dominion" (Rom. 5:10, AMP). This continual deliverance is facilitated by the power of the Holy Spirit operating in our lives.

6. *You are God's representative to the lost and dying world.*

In his second letter to the Corinthians, Paul describes the new creation as "ambassadors," pleading with men "for His sake to lay hold of the divine favor [now offered you] and be reconciled to God" (2 Cor. 5:20, AMP). Our mission is to reconnect the world to Him. Interestingly, the word *represent* literally means "to present the same thing once again."

As members of the body of Christ, we are here in this world with the mission of representing Jesus to our generation. This "representation" actually goes far beyond simply "acting on His behalf." It involves presenting Jesus to contemporary society in the same way that He was presented to Israel during His earthly life and ministry. As an ambassador of the kingdom, you are called to represent Him to those who are around you. That's why Paul also called us living epistles, seen and read of all men. (See 2 Corinthians 3:2–3.)

Your mission in life is to represent Jesus Christ as One who is relevant, compassionate and filled with righteousness, peace and joy. I am convinced that if this generation is going to come to faith in the God of the Bible, then it will be because they see modern men and women living in His presence, under His kingdom rule.

Society will never be changed because of a historical document. Believing in a historical figure will never transform the fallen nature of man. What men and women are in need of is for someone to show them the resurrected Christ, who is alive today, ruling the universe in wisdom, power and love.

7. Do not judge your future by the afflictions of your present.

If you had been an observer in Palestine during the life, death and burial of Jesus Christ, you would have never anticipated His redemptive impact upon the entire world. As a matter of fact, His very own disciples did not even anticipate the universal consequence of His personal actions. It was only after the Resurrection that everything became clear to them. And likewise, if you judge the success of your future based upon the light affliction of your present struggle, you will miss the exceeding weight of glory that is being formed within you.

BORN INTO ADOPTION

When the fullness of the time had come, God sent forth His Son, born of a woman, born under the law, to redeem those who were under the law, that we might receive the adoption as sons.

—GALATIANS 4:4–5

Having predestined us to adoption as sons by Jesus Christ to Himself, according to the good pleasure of His will.

—EPHESIANS 1:5

Not only were we born into the heavenly family, but we were also personally chosen and legally adopted by Jesus Christ. Our relationship as the new creation is so secure that Paul could ask the question, "Who can separate me from the love of Christ?", knowing full well the answer in advance. No one. Absolutely no one. You are in the process of becoming who you already are.

In between the Word
incarnate and the Word that became
institutionalized, the early church
operated in great power and glory.

Eleven

TRANSFORMING YOUR
THEOLOGY INTO BIOLOGY

W HEN THE IMAGE Maker came to earth in the
likeness of human flesh, He revealed the vast
difference between divine life and human life. Although
He lived as a man, He chose to live according to the
value system of heavenly life. Not only was Jesus born
from above, but He also drew His life source from above.
When He demonstrated the pattern for living, He
revealed to us the immense difference between those
things birthed of the Spirit and those things birthed of
the flesh.

This distinction was so vivid that there was no misunderstanding over the identity of His first-generation followers. They were reviled, persecuted, renounced and rejected, but they were never ignored. The separation between those who professed faith in Christ and those who did not was far more sharply defined than it is today. In the spiritual climate of this postmodern culture, we find it much easier to blend into our surroundings and to live life without provocation. But is it profitable? How can the world follow something than it cannot identify?

I am firmly convinced that those characteristics that distinguished the first-generation church from the unregenerate world were foundational issues rather than superficial ones. They didn't just live differently from the rest of culture—they *were fundamentally* different. They didn't just act different than the rest of society—at the core of their being they *were* different. It wasn't because they rode bicycles and wore white shirts with black pocket protectors that identified them as "Elder Peter" or "Apostle Paul." They were identified because they evidenced their new personhood with a brand-new lifestyle. These first-century Christians understood their distinction as the body of Christ. They were fully convinced of their essential identity and their ultimate destiny. And furthermore, they celebrated their uniqueness as the new creation.

You can learn to talk like a Christian, you can learn to act like a Christian and yet not really be a truly transformed "Christian"—just as you can talk Chinese, act Chinese, eat Chinese food and still be a Norwegian at heart! Your cosmetic presentation does not always evidence who you are on the inside. And the sad part about it is that at some point your presentation will wear thin, and who you really are will begin to leak out. (Actually, this breakdown usually happens under pressure, and you don't leak out—you explode!)

But these first-century believers didn't simply *act* like Christians—they *were* Christlike. They were in the process of "fleshing out" the Word of God on a daily basis. They had come to learn that theology was not something to be contained to the synagogue, the Promise Keepers' Rally or the Women's Aglow meeting. Their theology was in the process of becoming their biology.

Someone once coined the phrase, "Christians go to heaven, but disciples change the world." The difference between the two is that a disciple understands his or her identity. If we are the "generation upon whom the ends of the world are come," then it is vital that we come to faith regarding who we are and why we are alive.

INCARNATION OR INSTITUTION

THE LINE BETWEEN the believing and nonbelieving community was vividly distinct. The distinction between those who were Christians and those who were not was sharply defined. Far more defined, in fact, than it is today. In our postmodern culture it is quite possible to blend into our cultural surroundings as a "secret agent Christian," so that no one knows who you are but you. I've discovered that some Christians even work hard to hide their essential identity, like a CIA operative on a secret mission or a drug enforcement agent under cover. They have mastered the art of remaining undetected and undiscovered.

We can make excuses all day for why things are as they are. We can rely on time-worn excuses such as "the times have changed" or "there is a strong postmodern agenda working against us" or "the government is taking away our religious rights." But none of those excuses hold any water at all because of what we read in the New Testament. This generation of first-century Christians lived in changing times. They worshiped God in the midst of a pluralistic

191

society that rejected monotheism, embracing the manner of idol worship.

This first-generation upper-room community suffered under the oppression of an unjust Roman government and had their every move opposed by religious leaders. Yet in spite of every challenge that worked against them, they still turned the world upside down in just a few short years. So, as you can see, our excuses have no real validity.

I believe the real difference between first-century Christianity and Christianity in the twenty-first century is not found in society's attitude toward us; the real difference is found in whom we perceive ourselves to be. I often wonder if we are developing the same quality of Christians as were matured in the first century, or are we creating a generation high on style and low on substance? These are the church members Mario Murillo calls "high-maintenance, low-impact Christians."

In between the Word *incarnate* and the Word that became *institutionalized*, the first-century church existed in great power and glory. And by God's grace we can recapture the same quality of life and ministry—perhaps even greater. But it will only be through the personal embodiment of the Word in our lives. It will only be because we make the decision to live wholly unto Him.

The choice every generation has faced since the first-century church is found in 2 Corinthians 3, and it is this: Will we allow the Word to become *incarnate* or *institutionalized* in our lives? The choice is ours—letter or Spirit, institution or incarnate, epitaph or biography.

What biography has already begun to be written about you? What do your unsaved friends, coworkers or classmates think about when they hear your name? Have you demonstrated Jesus "with skin on" to them?

Transforming Your Theology Into Biology

Becoming an Everyday Christian

> The Word became flesh and blood, and *moved into the neighborhood.* We saw the glory with our own eyes, the one-of-a-kind glory, like Father, like Son, generous inside and out, true from start to finish.
> —JOHN 1:14, THE MESSAGE, EMPHASIS ADDED

The beginning point of this wonderful journey toward reconciliation was when the Word became flesh. The first step on the journey to reconciliation is incarnation. Before God could ever redeem fallen humanity, the Incarnation had to become more than a concept. It had to transcend a strategic plan of action; it had to be invested into humanity.

The radical nature of being an "everyday" Christian demands that you present your body a living sacrifice, refusing to be conformed to the spirit of the world, as you renew your mind to the revelation of God's perfect will for your life. In order to pursue the perfect will of God for your life, at some point you will have to expand your operative theology.

The more that I study the Scriptures, the more I am convinced that the Word of God contains a number of areas of critical concern that are never really addressed because we are afraid of the resulting implications. Deep down we know that if we really believe everything that this Book has to say, then we are going to have to be responsible to live in a way to which we have not yet surrendered. Jesus said, "To whom much is given, from him much will be required" (Luke 12:48). Yet the nature of religion is to settle for far less than we have been offered through the power of the gospel. Karl Barth scathingly indicted the theological community when he said, "The Word became flesh—and then through theologians, it became words again."[1]

As we grow in Christ, we tend to develop this internal navigational tool that carefully directs us around the hot spots in the Word of God in order to preserve self. The real problem with self-preservation is that you cannot preserve the image of self and that of Christ at the same time. Your heart cannot be both calloused and compassionate. You will either be ruled by the lusts of your flesh or by the Holy Spirit. It is impossible to live under law and grace. You cannot be a friend of sinners and of Pharisees. One image will ultimately rise up and dominate the other.

If you are ever going to make a difference in this world...if you are ever going to touch genuinely the life of even one person for eternity, it will happen because you made the decision to embody the gospel in order to demonstrate true Christlikeness!

IDENTIFY TO RECONCILE

BASED UPON HIS understanding of the essential identity of the new creation, Paul describes the mission of this newly regenerated people.

> Therefore, if anyone is in Christ, he is a new creation; old things have passed away; behold, all things have become new. Now all things are of God, who has reconciled us to Himself through Jesus Christ, and has given us the ministry of reconciliation, that is, that God was in Christ reconciling the world to Himself, not imputing their trespasses to them, and has committed to us the word of reconciliation.
>
> —2 CORINTHIANS 5:17–19

Because we have been reconciled, we are now the agents of reconciliation. Now follow this carefully, because I do not believe that the chronological order in which Paul speaks is incidental. The order in which this is written and portrayed is critical to a full understanding of our mission in life. We have been given the "ministry" of reconciliation—even before we were given the "word" of reconciliation.

These two words contain the key to our involvement in the ministry of reconciliation. Let me describe it like this. The Greek word for "ministry" is the word *diakonia* from which we derive the word *deacon*, better defined as a "servant or attendant." On the other hand, the Greek word *logos*, translated "word," literally means the "divine expression" or "the spoken word including the thought."

Paul says that following the *diakonia* of reconciliation, we have been given the *logos* of reconciliation. In other words, we are the servants of reconciliation long before we are the announcers of reconciliation. Only when we truly serve hurting humanity as instruments of reconciliation are we scripturally qualified to communicate the message of reconciliation.

You cannot reconcile what you have not served. The very nature of the word *reconciliation* denotes personal involvement, a life commitment. To *reconcile* is to "re-conciliate, to bring together opposing forces."

The nature of reconciliation requires a personal contact or an investment of one's life. This is the understanding of reconciliation that drove Jesus into contact with the broken, hurting outcasts of society. The ministry of reconciliation required that He become robed in the frailty of humanity. According to Isaiah 53, He was to be "numbered with the transgressors" (v. 12).

He could not reconcile all things back to the Father by sitting on an ivory throne in heaven, detached from the affairs of humanity. Jesus had to make contact with the woman at the well in order to reconcile her. He had to make contact with the thief on the cross in order to redeem him.

Consider the position of a hostage negotiator for a

moment. Before the hostage negotiator can reconcile the hostage with freedom, he will have to place himself in a position that may not be comfortable to him. It may even require stepping into a place of grave danger or personal risk. If necessary, he will place himself in an environment that isn't altogether friendly with his belief system.

Doesn't that sound exactly like what Jesus did when the woman at the well said to Him, "Don't you realize that you're a Jew and I'm a Samaritan, and this environment is hostile toward your identity?"

When Jesus walked the seashore of Galilee healing the brokenhearted and setting free the captive, He compassionately identified with the broken and the outcast. Yet He did not enter into the common experience that led them into their state of brokenness. He did not relate to them on the lowest common denominator.

True intercession is always born out of identification, which is not always common experience. Sometimes we confuse the two and end up with the warped perspective that we have to experience what others have experienced in order to effectively relate to them. Wrong! There is a difference between spiritual identification and common experience.

In other words, if you've messed up your life by committing adultery, I don't have to commit adultery in order to identify with the pain of what you are going through. We don't identify based upon a common experience; we identify based upon my compassionate concern for you.

Galatians 6:1 speaks of where our greatest identification should lie.

> Brethren, if a man is overtaken in any trespass, you who are spiritual restore such a one in a spirit of gentleness, considering yourself lest you also be tempted.

Your greatest identification should lie in being a son of

God. With that understanding, from that operational base of purity and power, you are enabled to reconcile others. The highest allegiance to which Jesus had dedicated His life was to grace and truth!

Identification is more than mere human sympathy; it is compassionate interaction. God has called us to *empathize* with the world, not to *sympathize* with the world. Mere human sympathy always produces spiritual weakness. But compassionate empathy releases grace to change lives.

You see, the first key to effectively reaching this generation is found in compassionately identifying with suffering humanity while at the same time not allowing ourselves to be overcome by the very things that are destroying them. Identification does not mean participation in the very thing that is destroying another.

I once read a story about a man crossing a bridge. As he casually glanced up, he was startled to see a man perched high on the steel girders preparing to jump. "Don't jump!" yelled the passerby.

"If you can give me three legitimate reasons to live, I won't jump," responded the suicidal man. After ten minutes of deep contemplation, the passerby climbed the girders and jumped with him!

The identification to which we are called is the ministry of helping suffering humanity off the bridge of destruction through compassionate interaction. We have seen too many Christians leap off the bridge in this generation because they did not understand how to identify without becoming overcome.

BE A CONTAGIOUS CHRISTIAN

THE SECOND KEY to developing the ministry of reconciliation is to become a contagious Christian. If we do not demonstrate a quality of life greater than that which the world already experiences, then where is the incentive for change? If our lives do not reflect the answers that Christ offers to the questions of secular man, then what are we really saying to society?

Are we saying that this "Jesus stuff" is really good if you're a loner or a loser? If our lives do not reflect the quality of kingdom living that He offers to us, then we are selling a product that we don't really believe in ourselves.

Some people have difficulty in evangelism because they don't really believe in the product. Instead of "hitting" the streets, they should be "hitting" the altars and coming to faith in Christ all over again. I've discovered that it's difficult to sell what you don't really believe in, because your life presentation lacks passion. Society is attracted to passionate people. Passionate people are contagious.

Most people find it easy to pursue their real passion in life when they discover what comes naturally to them and what they find fulfilling. Have you ever wondered why people choose certain careers? What motivates certain people to enter politics, law, medicine, aeronautics, quantum physics, computer programming or athletics? The driving force is passion. Likewise, why are some people more effective at evangelism than others? Passion!

Passionate people are persuasive. Passionate people are contagious. Passionate people are effective. Society will never be truly transformed by "drive-by shoutings" or "gospel muggings," but it will be transformed by seeing people who live out the great adventure of the gospel.

DEMONSTRATING THE MESSAGE

THE REAL CHALLENGE we encounter in our postmodern culture is to make Christ attractive to all men. By that, I don't mean to imply that He needs us as public relations people to perk up His image in a fallen world...to launch a clever ad campaign that reflects His brilliance. The way we make Christ attractive to all men is by simply allowing Him to shine forth the beauty of His resurrected life through us. Jesus said, "If you'll lift Me up, I'll do the real work here." (See John 12:32.) Our responsibility is to present the person of Christ with passion and compassion, and He will draw men near.

As much as the unbelieving world would like to understand the true identity of the church, they cannot, for they are spiritually blind. The unregenerate man is incapable of understanding the theology of incarnation, which only leaves him with the picture of our demonstration. They have taken the same position as many others in first-century Palestine who refused to acknowledge Jesus as the Messiah and yet were drawn to Him because of His miracles. They did not understand how He could be God in the flesh, but they were attracted to His character qualities as a peacemaker and a champion of the downtrodden, the hurting and the outcast.

Even though the world may not understand your theological identity as a son of God, they will know you by your fruit. And when they see your good works, they will glorify your Father in heaven (Matt. 5:16). When you let the light of honesty and integrity shine to your friends in corporate America, then you have given them an invitation to glorify the Father. When you raise sons and daughters who love God and serve the kingdom, then you have given your neighborhood an invitation to glorify the Father in heaven. When you let the light of a joyful, peaceful home shine to your lost family members, you have given them an invitation to glorify the Father. And even if they don't understand your identity, they will at least consider your demonstration.

The Image Maker specializes in
restructuring the distorted images
we see around us in society. Wise
beyond comprehension, He is infinitely
patient when it comes to the spiritual,
emotional and physical development of
the image bearer.

Twelve

TRANSFORMING
THE MISINFORMED

DO YOU KNOW who you really are? Do you understand the purpose for which you were born? It seems far easier for most of us to imitate the life of another than it is truly to live our own. When we find ourselves living under the shadow of a dominant personality, such as a father, mother, husband, teacher or pastor, many people have the tendency to assume the identity of that personality rather than processing through the journey to discover whom God created them to be. We are far better at *imitating* than we are at simply *being*.

Before I take you any further, a brief qualification is in order. I believe in spiritual mentoring. As the father of three sons and the spiritual overseer of an international network of churches (CitiNet International), I am privileged to serve as a spiritual coach to a number of strong young men. Furthermore, I am fully aware of the words of Paul, who set the pattern for spiritual mentoring when he boldly stated, "Follow my example, as I follow the example of Christ" (1 Cor. 11:1, NIV). On another occasion he said, "Therefore I urge you, imitate me" (1 Cor. 4:16). There is a fine line between impressing those I oversee with the image of God vs. impressing them with my own personality.

Spiritual control is one full step beyond true biblical authority. So many times, we see domination and control in ministry because of unresolved insecurity in the life of the one leading. True spiritual mentoring requires that the coach settle any unresolved issues in his or her life before attempting to significantly shape the lives of others. When a mentor has unresolved expectations within his or her life, that person stands in danger of projecting himself on the life of the one being mentored.

As the model Father, The Image Maker has only our best interest at heart. He is not living in disappointment while waiting on someone to assume His unfulfilled goals. He wants what is best for us even when His work isn't accomplished as quickly as He would like for it to be. God would rather see you plodding along, spiritually healthy, toward the fulfillment of His will than to see you race forward while spiritually anemic and susceptible to spiritual infirmity. Walking with integrity is more important than running with impatience! He is more concerned about your state of being than your performance.

The Image Maker specializes in restructuring the distorted images we see around us in society. Wise beyond comprehension, He is infinitely patient when it comes to the spiritual, emotional and physical development of the image bearer. He is not restricted to one single method of restoration and will use any means within His infinite grasp to rebuild the broken ruins of our lives. No vessel is marred so greatly that the Master Potter cannot repair and restore it back to useful service.

TRANSFORMING THE MISINFORMED

I WANT US to examine the lives of several prominent biblical characters as they made the journey from misinformation to transformation. As we do, let's honestly examine their strengths and weaknesses. Oftentimes we perceive these biblical figures to be about as one dimensional as the black ink on the pages of our Bibles. In doing so, we miss the complexity of the human drama that unfolds in every chapter and verse.

Moses

Given up for adoption and raised in an environment foreign to his essential identity, Moses struggled to understand his purpose in life. Using a creative ability beyond my own, Steven Spielberg recently presented an image of Moses that is both intriguing and compelling.

One of the interesting angles presented in *The Prince of Egypt* involved the emotional entanglement that Moses must have had with the household of Pharaoh. After all, it was the daughter of Pharaoh who spared his life when she drew him out of the bulrushes. For forty years Moses lived in the house of the king, enjoying the privilege of honor and wealth. Acts 7:22 says, "Moses was learned in all the wisdom of the Egyptians, and was mighty in words and deeds." Through the writings of Josephus we discover that his education consisted of the mysteries of the Egyptian religion, arithmetic, geometry, poetry, music, medicine and hieroglyphics. Moses was eventually promoted to the rank of general of the Egyptian armies. His life must have been intertwined with Egyptian culture.

But at forty years of age, something deep in the recesses of his soul began crying out for more. Maybe it was a faint impression from his childhood that he could not shake. Perhaps it was a memory of his mother guiding him down the path toward the one true and living God. This may be the first picture of a man encountering a major midlife crisis. But rather than buying a fiery red sports chariot and a silly little diamond stud in his ear, Moses began to ask the question, "How does my past relate to my future?" To ignore the past is to stagnate the present.

After four decades of absence, Moses made his first pilgrimage back to the tents of Israel. And somewhere between the luxury of Egypt and the squalor of Israel, he crossed a line from which he could not return. Hebrews 11:24–26 says:

> By faith Moses, when he was come to years, refused to be called the son of Pharaoh's daughter; choosing rather to suffer affliction with the people of God, than to enjoy the pleasure of sin for a season; esteeming the reproach of Christ greater riches than the treasures in Egypt: for he had respect unto the recompense of the reward.
>
> —KJV

With half of his life completed, Moses began the search to discover who he truly was. Through a series of encounters with the great "I AM," he began to see whom The Image Maker had created him to be.

Abraham

When Abram received the prophetic word that he was

going to be the father of a son, he was already seventy-five years old and beginning to feel the effects of a lifetime spent in the desert. His wife, Sarai, was also past the age of childbearing. As a matter of fact, she had been barren her entire life. In their minds, Abram and Sarai saw themselves as an aging, childless couple without any hope for an heir. They were bound with an image of barrenness. Abram had already made plans to leave his entire estate to his servant Eliezar of Damascus.

That's why The Image Maker gave Abram more than a verbal promise. In Genesis 15, God took him out under the stars, and said, "Take a look at the heavens, *tell* the stars if you are able to number them, so shall your seed be." (See Genesis 15:5, KJV, emphasis added). What was God doing on this prophetic field trip? He was replacing Abram's image of barrenness with the image of abundance. He was burning a new image of prosperity into the soul of Abram. As strange as it sounds, The Image Maker instructed him *to talk to the stars.*

Can you imagine Abram speaking to the stars, saying, "One day I will be able to match you son for star"? Can you imagine this patriarch lying awake in his tent at night trying to picture the face of his long-awaited son? Throughout this long exhausting process, an image of victory is beginning to form in the soul of Abram.

The pattern by which this image was formed in the soul of Abram is not incidental. The inner image was formed when Abram made the decision to confirm the promise with his mouth. Words have a significant impact upon our self-image. This principle operates to our benefit or to our destruction, depending upon how we use it. As you speak, your mind is being renewed by the power of words. So when you fill your environment with words of unbelief, your mind begins to believe it, and you find yourself powerless to accomplish the very thing you desire the most. You have renewed your mind to an image of defeat.

The real problem with most of us is that we have never worked long enough on establishing an inner image of victory deep in our soul (mind, will, emotions). We spend most of our time thinking about what we cannot accomplish in life for whatever reason we believe that we cannot accomplish it.

Now, let's flash forward two decades in Abram's life. Following the original promise, God has only mentioned His promise of the seed twice to Abram. The first occasion was just after Lot separated from him, choosing the well-watered plains of Mamre over his relationship with Abram. The second occasion was just after he paid tithes to Melchizedek, king of Salem.

Abram only received two confirmations during the twenty-four year period from the promise to the product. And yet many Christians struggle with insecurity concerning their destiny if God doesn't reassure them on a weekly basis. I wonder if you are prepared to walk in faith concerning the promise of your inheritance, even if you don't receive another confirmation for twelve years?

Yet in spite of this prolonged silence, Abram staggers not at the promise of God through unbelief, but was strong in faith. Even when he took matters into his own hands with Hagar, he wasn't struggling with God's *promise*—he was wrestling with God's *timing*.

When the image starts to grow dim, God replaces it with a greater image by changing Abram's and Sarai's names. *Abram* literally means "exalted father," but *Abraham* is defined as "the father of many nations." *Sarah*, the feminine form of *Sar*, means "princess" or "mother of a prince." Every time this childless couple hears the name *Abraham* or *Sarah*, they are in essence hearing "Daddy" or "Mama." God is reconstructing Abraham's inner image into one of victory. Before God could even get Abraham into prosperity, God had to get prosperity into Abraham. Before God could bring Abraham into prosperity of substance, God had to first bring him into prosperity of soul.

He did this by working on the vision of his self-image. God began to unlock the power of Abraham's righteous imagination. According to Romans 4:17, this is the process of calling "those things which do not exist as though they did." Let me ask you a simple question: What are imaginations? They are images! They are pictures painted on the canvas of our memories by thoughts. Thought pictures.

Your imagination is a God-ordained tool that can and should be used for the sake of righteousness in the earth. Even though power-hungry pagans have perverted this ability, your imagination is not an evil thing. Always remember, the devil is an *imitator*, not an *originator*. As an impersonator, his mission is to steal righteous things and distort them for his own purposes. The destructive pattern by which he works is to usurp, pervert, distort and then import this deviation into a generation.

This supernatural ability isn't something that was given to man by the devil; it was placed in man by God. In Genesis 1:26, God Himself said, "Let Us make man in Our *image*, according to Our likeness; let them have dominion..." (emphasis added). I believe God had a "mental" picture of the finished product before He ever began the process.

Those imaginations that *are* wrong (even dangerous) are the ones that exalt themselves *against* the knowledge of God. But once you have come to the knowledge of the will of God, then you have the right to use your imagination in order for His purpose to be fulfilled in your life.

Our lack of understanding concerning this vital aspect of faith is the very thing that keeps us from breaking forth into the reality of the Abrahamic Covenant. If you want to walk in the blessing of Abraham, which has become ours in Christ Jesus, then you have to learn how to *see* it *before* you see it. When you really begin to see it in the spirit before you ever see it in the natural, then nothing will be restrained from you.

I believe that God is looking for people who will spend enough time in His Word and in His presence to affect what they see on the inside of them. That's why you're not wasting time when you are hearing, memorizing and confessing the Word of God, because as you do these things you are working on the inner image that God is trying to create in your inner man.

God wants to make the inner image of victory so vivid and distinct that when you close your eyes you see yourself in victory. When you lay down to sleep, you dream about victory. When you awake in the morning, you awake into victory. If you walk out of your company with a pink slip in your hand, you walk out in victory looking for bigger and better things. When the enemy knocks you down, God wants you to see the potential for victory in the stars circling your head. When you come to that level of faith, you are one step away from the manifestation of the promise.

Abraham spent his entire life looking for something he had already seen. Even when it came to the sacrifice of his son, he used the brush of faith to paint an image of the resurrection of Isaac on the canvas of his soul! He saw this young man blessing the nations. He saw his promised seed as innumerable as the stars in the heavens and the grains of sand on the seashore. He saw the final product even before the journey began.

Jacob

On the very first occasion in the Scriptures in which Jacob introduces himself, he does so in the name of Esau, his twin brother. Masquerading behind the hairy skin of a kid goat, with the connivance of his mother, Jacob manipulates his father into imparting the family blessing to him. He accomplishes this deceptive ruse by assuming the name of Esau. But even though he receives the father's blessing, he still lacks the father's favor. It seems to me that he probably wanted the blessing even more than the inheritance.

Jacob clearly struggled with his relationship with his father from the beginning. When these twins were born, Esau came out first, bright red, with a full mustache and beard, a bow in one hand and a fishing rod in the other, and his father said, "I like him! This is my kind of man." But Jacob came out second, holding onto Esau's heel with one hand, playing the violin with the other. And Isaac said, "That is a mama's boy! I'll take the first one, and mama can have the other one."

Perhaps you grew up in a home just like that one. You were born to wounded parents, who in turn wounded you with rejection and abandonment. And you have repeated that same cycle of failure with your children. As John Maxwell says, "Hurting people hurt people."

From his earliest days, Jacob evidently thought that the only way to succeed was by being somebody else. At this stage in his life, Jacob is still wrestling with the inner issue of his essential identity. I believe he is struggling with insecurity because he lacked the affirmation of his father. Genesis 25:28 reveals the tensions found present in this family when it declares, "And Isaac loved Esau because he ate of his game, but Rebekah loved Jacob." The implication is clear that Isaac showed favoritism toward his first son while leaving his second son to be loved by his mother. Very seldom is one raised in this kind of environment without experiencing the scars of rejection.

Jacob was uncomfortable with himself. He wasn't happy

to be who he was. His history is filled with failure and disappointment. He had been overlooked by his father, manipulated by his mother, rejected by his brother and cheated by his father-in-law. He married an ugly woman while romancing a beauty. His life was filled with as many twists and turns as any ridiculous soap opera. Throughout his life, only one thing remained constant: Jacob wasn't happy to be Jacob.

But you have to be you to be blessed of God. Our problem today is that we want to be somebody else, anybody else, just as long as we are not forced to be ourselves. As I said in an earlier chapter, we find ourselves in a society where we are far better at *imitating* than we actually are at simply *being*.

We finally discover Jacob sitting alone beside the brook Jabbok. "Then Jacob was left alone; and a Man wrestled with him until the breaking of day" (Gen. 32:24).

Notice carefully that Jacob was not necessarily alone by choice; he was alone by divine arrangement. The Scripture declares, "Then Jacob was *left* alone...." As painful as it is, God will often use isolation to prepare you for a visitation. Sometimes God cannot draw near to us because of the crowd. He cannot break into our consciousness because there is no room for Him to dwell. We have filled up our lives with activity but no destiny; we have cluttered our minds with the cares of life and have left no room for the Author of life. When you find yourself in that state, God carefully pulls back the crowd and leaves you wondering where the party went.

God will even allow people to leave you to test your response to being alone. You see, there is a difference between *being alone* and being *lonely*. Some people have such a fear of being lonely that they fill up their lives with meaningless activity and unprofitable relationships, because after all, anything is better than being lonely. But you can be lonely in a crowd. *Being alone* is a physical position, but *being lonely* is an emotional and spiritual position. Most people who are afraid of being alone are uncomfortable with themselves.

I believe this picture in the life of Jacob was eventually played out in the life of the prodigal son, who actually wanted the favor of his father more than his inheritance. That's why, after squandering his inheritance, he came back home to his father, knowing full well that there was no more inheritance to receive. The only thing left for him was the thing that he really wanted the most—the unconditional love and affirmation of his father.

And there by the brook in the gray light of the dawn, following the most intense wrestling match of his entire life, the Man said, "Your name shall no longer be called Jacob, but Israel; for you have struggled with God and with men, and have prevailed" (Gen. 32:28). In one moment of time, after a lifetime of futility, God unveiled Jacob's essential identity, and he discovered whom he was created to be.

Peter

Simon loved Jesus more than anything else in the world. Yet at times his unbroken will was in conflict with the One he loved and served. After walking with Jesus for two and one-half years, during a monumental burst of revelation he realized that Jesus of Nazareth was the Son of the living God.

Jesus responded to his revelation by unveiling his essential identity.

> Jesus came back, "God bless you, Simon, son of Jonah! . . . And now, I'm going to tell you who you are, *really* are. You are Peter, a rock."
> —MATTHEW 16:17–18, THE MESSAGE

This Galilean fisherman, who had defined his own life by his impetuous nature, his unbroken will and his unbridled tongue, was actually "The Rock." In order for Simon to fulfill his ultimate destiny as the prophet of Pentecost, Jesus had to unveil his essential identity.

When Simon came to faith in who he was in light of the grace of God, he was transformed from being a fragmented stone to a building block in the kingdom of God. He went from being a "zero" to a "hero" because of the revelation of his worth and value in the eyes of the One he loved most.

Paul

Saul of Tarsus had such a revolutionary identity change that he eventually said, "The old me is no longer alive; a new man has replaced him." Struck down by the power of God as he rode to Damascus on his mission to murder those who had abandoned the orthodoxy of the Jewish religion in favor of following Jesus of Nazareth, Saul found himself blind and confused for three long days. In fasting and prayer, he cried out to know the will of God for his life, and the revelation that came to him unveiled his essential identity.

Assuaging the fears of Ananias who had been sent to minister to Saul, the Lord said unto him, "Go, for he [Saul] is a chosen vessel of Mine to bear My name before Gentiles, kings, and the children of Israel" (Acts 9:15). One writer put it this way: "The power of God hit Saul of Tarsus so hard on the road to Damascus that it knocked the 'S' off the front of his name, replaced it with a 'P,' and he became Paul. His name changed, his identity changed and his nature changed."[1]

Josiah

In 2 Chronicles, we find the story of an eight-year-old boy king by the name of Josiah who was brought to the throne in the midst of a national civil war. In the eighth year of his reign, he began the process of tearing down every false image and breaking the power of every unrighteous idol in the land (2 Chron. 34:3–7). Eighteen years into his very successful reign, he reached a significant turning point in his leadership. After purging the nation, Josiah began the daunting task of rebuilding the temple (vv. 8–13).

Evidently this mission sprang out of a personal epiphany when Josiah looked around one day and said, "The idols are gone, and the powers of darkness have been eradicated from the land, but the house of the Lord has not been restored." He sent for two significant men in the kingdom, Hilkiah the high priest and Shaphan the scribe, who began to direct the restoration process. As they were digging through the ruins one day, they discovered the Book of the Law, which had been lost for several generations (vv. 14–16). In doing so, they rediscovered the destiny of Israel.

Hilkiah was so excited about their discovery that he immediately took it to Josiah, who began to read the glory of God's Word. And when this twenty-six-year-old king discovered the essential identity of his people, he discovered his ultimate destiny in the history of Israel.

When this young king saw himself in the book, everything in his world was rocked. Everything in his world began the process of conforming to who he was. He no longer walked according to the course that had been prescribed to him by advisors and counselors. Josiah broke out of the image being imposed upon his life, and he began to live according to the power of an inner revelation of his essential identity.

Cyrus

My final example is found in Ezra 1. After seventy years of Babylonian captivity, Babylon was overthrown by the power of Medo-Persia, which became the ruling power. After this transition, the reign of King Cyrus was ushered in. One day, a scribe came to him with the writings of the Prophets. Although we are not certain of the identity of this unnamed scribe, popular legend says it was probably Daniel. This perceptive scribe asked the question that radically altered Cyrus's destiny, "Have you seen your name in the Book?" Although King Cyrus was following a course of natural lineage, God had something greater for him than the image of his father.

At that moment, the scribe took him back to the words of the prophet, prophetically written two hundred years earlier, declaring, "[Cyrus] is My shepherd, and he shall perform all My pleasure" (Isa. 44:28). When King Cyrus saw his name in the Book, he embraced his destiny and radically altered the course of human history.

Is Your Name in the Book?

FOR YEARS I read the Bible as a historical document about mighty heroes and peculiar customs. Although the Bible nourished me spiritually, it had very little impact upon the way I viewed my life and pursued my destiny. All of that changed when I discovered my name in the Book. In case you're suddenly wondering what version I'm presently reading, let me make it clear. No, my personal name cannot be found in the Scriptures. But my identity in Christ can be found. My destiny as the new creation is clearly present. My name is in the Book. Your name is in the Book! But you must have eyes to see it.

The beauty of the Word of God is that when we really come to terms with who we are in the family of God, we begin to see ourselves in the Book. When I read about Paul the Apostle, I'm not just reading about Paul; I'm reading about the same potential found present in Terry Michael Crist, Jr. When I see the signs and the wonders and the exploits of the New Testament church, I'm not reading ancient history; I'm reading living reality. When you discover the reality of your identity in Christ, everything in your world begins the process of conforming to who you are.

Have you seen your name in the Book? For those who are searching, you will find your identity in the same Book that Jesus did. Although He was fully God, He laid aside His deity when He became a man, and in His humanity, He had to study the Scriptures to discover who He was.

> The Spirit of the LORD is upon Me, because He has anointed Me to preach the gospel to the poor; He has sent Me to heal the brokenhearted, to proclaim liberty to the captives and recovery of sight to the blind, to set at liberty those who are oppressed.
> —LUKE 4:18

Following His baptism in the Jordan River at the hands of John the Baptist, Jesus heard a voice from heaven confirming His essential identity. When Jesus came to faith in who He was, nothing could stand in His way. Likewise, when you come to faith in who you are in Christ, nothing shall effectively withstand you.

Perhaps you have been duped into believing the misinformation that has been disseminated by the enemy in his desperate attempt to deceive you into believing that you are less than God created you to be. The time has come to shake yourself free from insignificance and insecurity once and for all. As a child of God, you occupy the highest position in the universe, just under The Image Maker Himself. You have ultimate worth and value. Believe it!

> To him who overcomes I will give some of the hidden manna to eat. And I will give him a white stone, and on the stone a new name written which no one knows except him who receives it.
> —REVELATION 2:17

Notes

Before documenting these quotes borrowed from other sources, a brief qualification is in order. Although I have attempted to present each quote in light of the context in which it was written, please do not assume that every author noted here is in complete agreement with the position I have taken on these varying issues. While some of these authors have taken opposing views, their material was vital to my research and the development of this text. I offer my humble gratitude to each of these writers for helping to shape my perspective on the principles contained within this book. My life is forever changed because of you.

—THE AUTHOR

INTRODUCTION

1. William James, *The Principles of Psychology* (Cambridge: Harvard University Press, 1893), volume 1, chapter 10.

CHAPTER ONE
HOW IN THE WORLD DID WE GET HERE?

1. Jewel Kilcher, "Hands," copyright © 1998 WB Music Corp./Wiggly Tooth Music, ASCAP.
2. *Newsweek*, April 26, 1999, International Edition, "Why the Young Kill." Emblazoned across the cover of the May 3, 1999 U.S. Edition of *TIME Magazine* was the question *"Why?" TIME Magazine*, May 3, 1999, volume 153, no. 17, "What Can the Schools Do?" Emblazoned across the May 3, 1999 cover of *U.S. News and World Report* was the question *"Why?"*
3. Quoted in Walter Truett Anderson, *Reality Isn't What It Used to Be: Theatrical Politics, Ready-to-Wear Religion,*

Global Myths, Primitive Chic, and Other Wonders of the Post-modern World (San Francisco: Harper & Row, 1990), 51.

4. Chuck Colson, *Burden of Truth* (Wheaton: Tyndale House Publishers, Inc, 1997), 196.

5. Anthony Hoekema, *Created in God's Image*, (Grand Rapids: William B. Eerdmans Publishing Company, 1986), 2.

6. Tom Stoppard quote taken from Internet search on "creation-evolution" quotes.

7. George Gaylord Simpson, *The Meaning of Evolution* (New Haven: Yale University Press, 1971), 345.

8. Joseph Stalin, *Works* (Moscow and London: 1952/3), vol. 1, p. 304. Cited in Wetter, *Dialectical Materialism*, 325.

9. Ibid.

10. Gene Edward Veith, Jr., *Postmodern Times* (Wheaton: Crossway Books, 1994), 75.

11. Ravi Zacharias, *Shepherding a Soul-Less Culture* (Atlanta: Just Thinking, Spring/Summer 1999), 2.

12. Philip Yancey, *Finding God in Unexpected Places* (Ann Arbor: Vine Books, 1997), 145.

CHAPTER TWO
DISCOVERING THE DIVINE DESIGN

1. Quoted in Yancey, *Finding God in Unexpected Places*, 115.

2. Myles Munroe, *Understanding Your Potential* (Shippens-burg: Destiny Image Publishers, 1991), 23.

3. *Against Heresies, V.6.1, in Ante-Nicene Fathers*, vol. 1, ed. Alexander Roberts and James Donaldson (Grand Rapids: Eerdmans, 1953), 532.

4. *Vine's Complete Expository Dictionary of Biblical Words* (Nashville: Thomas Nelson, 1985), s.v. "image."

5. Ibid., s.v. "likeness."

6. *Dakes Annotated Reference Bible* (Lawerenceville, GA:

Notes

Dakes Bible Sales, 1963), p. 2, col. 1, note c.

7. Herman Bavinck, *Dogmatiek*, 2:566 as quoted in Hoekema, *Created in God's Image*.
8. Hoekema, *Created in God's Image*, 77.

CHAPTER THREE

THE LONG JOURNEY HOME

1. David Needham, *Birthright* (Sisters, OR: Multnomah Publishers, Inc., 1999), 30.
2. Bavinck, *Dogmatiek*, 3:137, as quoted in Hoekema, *Created in God's Image*.
3. Yancey, *Finding God in Unexpected Places*, 33.
4. C. S. Lewis, *The Problem of Pain* (New York: Macmillian, 1948), 70–71.
5. Emil Brunner, *Man in Revolt*, trans. Olive Wyon (New York: Scribner, 1939), 105.

CHAPTER FOUR

BACK TO EDEN AND BEYOND

1. A. W. Tozer, *The Divine Conquest* (Wheaton: Tyndale House, 1950), 22.
2. Philip Yancey and Dr. Paul Brand, *Fearfully and Wonderfully Made* (Grand Rapids: Zondervan, 1980), 46.
3. Ibid., 46.
4. Needham, *Birthright*, 62.
5. "Can Animals Think?" *TIME Magazine*, September 6, 1999, volume 154, No. 10.
6. Leon Morris, *The Gospel According to John* (Grand Rapids: Eerdmans, 1971), 212–213.
7. J. Knox Chamblin, *Paul and Self, Apostolic Teaching for Personal Wholeness* (Grand Rapids: Baker House Books, 1993), 85.

8. Arthur Custance, *Man in Adam and in Christ*, 3 vols. (Grand Rapids: Zondervan, 1975), 3:343–44. The author is using the word *species* in a broad sense and not a biological one.

CHAPTER FIVE
AWAKEN TO RIGHTEOUSNESS

1. Brunner, *Man in Revolt*, 501.
2. Al Novak, *Hebrew Honey* (Houston: J. Countryman Publishers, 1965), 221.
3. James Strong, *The New Strongs Exhaustive Concordance of the Bible* (Nashville: Thomas Nelson, 1995), s.v. 1343.
4. Johannes Behm "Kainos," *Theological Dictionary of the New Testament*, vol. 3. Ed. Gerhard Kittle (Grand Rapids: Eerdmans, 1965), 449.
5. Needham, *Birthright*, 132.
6. Yancey, Brand, *Fearfully and Wonderfully Made*, 47.

CHAPTER SIX
BECOMING WHO YOU ALREADY ARE

1. Robert McGee, *The Search for Significance* (Nashville: Word Publishing, 1998), 113.
2. Ernest L. Richert, *Freedom Dynamics* (Big Bear Lake, CA: The Thinker, 1977), ix.
3. A. J. Gordon, *In Christ, The Believer's Union With His Lord* (Sanford: Wade Pickren Publications, 1983), 2.
4. Isaac Asimov, *Journey Across the Subatomic Cosmos* (New York: Truman Talley Books, 1992), 235.
5. Myles Munroe, *The Pursuit of Purpose* (Shippensburg: Destiny Image, 1992), 31.

Notes

CHAPTER SEVEN
UNVEILING YOUR ESSENTIAL IDENTITY

1. Bruce Narramore, *Freedom From Guilt* (Eugene, OR: Harvest House, 1974), 90.
2. McGee, *The Search for Significance*, 55.
3. Ibid., 59.
4. Taken from live satellite seminar, *Worldwide Lessons in Leadership*, 1996, sponsored by the University of Tulsa, Tulsa, OK.

CHAPTER EIGHT
THE TECHNOLOGY OF THE NEW CREATION

1. Leonard Sweet, *Soul Tsunami* (Grand Rapids: Zondervan, 1999), 29.
2. William White, *The Theological and Grammatical Phrasebook of the Bible* (Chicago: Moody Press, 1984), 58, 96.
3. "Were You There When They Crucified My Lord?" author unknown, public domain.

CHAPTER NINE
LIVING FREE FROM SIN CONSCIOUSNESS

1. E. W. Kenyon, *Two Kinds of Righteousness* (n.p.: Kenyon's Gospel Publishing Society, Inc., 1996), 9.
2. Oliver Sacks, *An Anthropologist on Mars* (New York: Vintage Books, 1995), 113–114.
3. Tozer, *The Divine Conquest*, 29.
4. *The Discovery Bible, New American Standard New Testament, Referenced Edition. H.E.L.P.S.—The Study System of the Discovery Bible* (Chicago: Moody Press, 1987), xviii.

CHAPTER TEN
INVITING THE INCARNATION

1. Condensed and modernized from *St. Athanasisus on the Incarnation. Christianity Today*, Christian History, July/August 1996. Issue 51, vol. XV, no. 3, page 16.

2. J. I. Packer, *Christianity Today*, April 5, 1999, vol. 43, no. 4, page 70.

3. Condensed and modernized from *St. Athanasisus on the Incarnation.*

4. Reid, Virkler, Langstaff, Laine, *Seduction? A Biblical Response* (New Wilmington: Son-Rise Publications, 1986), 5.

5. F. J. Huegel, *Bone of His Bone* (Grand Rapids: Zondervan, n.d.), 13.

6. Quoted in Tim Hansel, *Holy Sweat* (Dallas: Word Publishing, n.d.), 29.

CHAPTER ELEVEN
TURNING YOUR THEOLOGY INTO BIOLOGY

1. Mario Murillo, *Fresh Fire* (Danville, CA: Anthony Douglas Publishing), 15.

2. Quoted in Hansel, *Holy Sweat*, 26.

CHAPTER TWELVE
TRANSFORMING THE MISINFORMED

1. Mark Hankins, *Taking Your Place in Christ* (Alexandria: Mark Hankins Ministries Publishing, 1996), 53.

Terry Crist has other books, audio and video product available. To obtain a catalog or to request more information about his church, apostolic network or ministry, please contact:

TERRY CRIST
SpiritBuilder Seminars and Resources
P.O. Box 8339
Scottsdale, AZ 85252

(480) 661-9209

Or visit his Web site at www.terrycrist.com

You can experience more of *God's grace & love!*

*I*f you would like free information on how you can know God more deeply and experience His grace, love and power more fully in your life, simply write or e-mail us. We'll be delighted to send you information that will be a blessing to you.

To check out other titles from **Creation House** that will impact your life, be sure to visit your local Christian bookstore, or call this toll-free number:

1-800-599-5750

For free information from Creation House:

CREATION HOUSE
600 Rinehart Rd.
Lake Mary, FL 32746
www.creationhouse.com

Your Walk With God Can Be Even Deeper...

With *Charisma* magazine, you'll be informed and inspired by the features and stories about what the Holy Spirit is doing in the lives of believers today.

Each issue:

- Brings you exclusive world-wide reports to rejoice over.
- Keeps you informed on the latest news from a Christian perspective.
- Includes miracle-filled testimonies to build your faith.
- Gives you access to relevant teaching and exhortation from the most respected Christian leaders of our day.

Call 1-800-829-3346 for 3 FREE trial issues
Offer #AOACHB

If you like what you see, then pay the invoice of $22.97 (**saving over 51% off the cover price**) and receive 9 more issues (12 in all). Otherwise, write "cancel" on the invoice, return it, and owe nothing.

Charisma Offer #AOACHB
P.O. Box 420234
Palm Coast, Florida 32142-0234
www.charismamag.com